Hardy Ger

G000256498

for the G(

Revised and enlarg

The material for this booklet has been provided by members of the Hardy Geranium Group of the Hardy Plant Society, to whom we are deeply grateful. Joy Jones would like to thank Judith Bradshaw, Jenny Fuller, Jenny Spiller and David Victor for their help and advice.

Line drawings by Peggy Dawe.
Silhouettes by Joy Jones.

Key to front cover.

1.   *G. himalayense* 'Irish Blue'
2.   *G. clarkei* 'Kashmir White'
3.   *G. pyrenaicum*
4.   *G. sanguineum*
5.   *G. harveyi*
6.   *G. caffrum*
7.   *G. 'Joy'*
8.   *G. robertianum*
9.   *G. pulchrum*
10. *G. robustum*
11. *G. hayatanum*

Edited and typeset by George Parker
Consultant editor to the Booklet Series: Tony Lord
First edition June 1992; Second edition April 1993; This edition January, 2001
© The Hardy Plant Society
ISBN 0 901687 17 0

Geranium 'Nimbus'

Introduction
JOY JONES

TO MANY PEOPLE, the name geranium still relates to the exotic, tender bedding plants, so popular in the Victorian era, which are now botanically, *Pelargonium*. Old habits die hard and so there is a lot of confusion when 'hardy geraniums' are mentioned. It is with these, the true *Geranium* or cranesbill (referring to the beak-like seed structure) that we are concerned in this booklet.

To confuse matters further, there are a few geraniums that are not entirely hardy in the British Isles. Nevertheless, the majority are able to withstand the coldest winters, easy to grow, practically disease-free, usually ignored by pests, tolerant of different soil conditions and able to thrive in sun or half shade (some deep shade).

Newcomers to gardening are well advised to start with some of the 'easy' species, in the probability that they will then be encouraged to collect more varieties. My first introduction to gardening was on heavy blue clay (adjoining the local brick fields). Everything I planted rotted or was devoured by slugs or smothered by pernicious weeds - until someone gave me *Geranium* x *magnificum*, which did so well I was soon on the road to geranium addiction.

Although some species have been grown in our gardens for over four hundred years, recently their popularity has greatly increased. Today the choice is very much wider and discerning gardeners are realising that there is a geranium for every situation. They are ideal for informal cottage gardens, but equally at home in more formal plantings. Their leaves (which press well for close examination) vary in shape, size and texture; some are pleasantly aromatic, though herb Robert, *G. robertianum*, is not so fragrant. It is, perhaps, the simplicity of the flowers that makes cranesbills so appealing and their ability to mingle delightfully with other plants.

You may ask if they have any disadvantages. One, possibly, is the profusion with which some species disperse their seedlings; this can be a problem, especially in small gardens. However, once you have learned to recognise the seedlings, unwanted ones are easily removed when small. If you have ground to spare, these can be grown on, just in case you have an exciting new hybrid. Another complaint is that some become untidy after the main flush of flowers, particularly *G. endressii* and *G.* x *oxonianum* and their forms. Shearing the foliage to the ground is the answer, resulting in a fresh crop of foliage and flowers, though watering in dry weather is advisable after this treatment.

Getting to know geraniums is an enjoyable pastime. Many can be seen by visiting specialist nurseries and botanic gardens. There is a National Collection of species and primary hybrids at Cambridge Botanic Garden, Cory Lodge, Bateman Street, Cambridge, and cultivars can be seen at Cherry Hinton Hall nearby. Further National Collections are held by Judith Bradshaw at Catforth Gardens near Preston; by Andrew Norton at New House Barn, Barrington, Ilminster, Somerset (*species*); and by D Browne at Coombland Gardens, Coneyhurst, Billingshurst, Sussex (*cultivars*).

Literature on geraniums is scarce. The late Margery Fish stimulated interest with her books, such as *Ground Cover Plants, Gardening in the Shade* and *Cottage Garden Flowers*. *Hardy Geraniums* by Dr Peter Yeo of Cambridge University was first published in 1985, after many years of research into the genus. This authoritative work has clarified the confusion surrounding previous naming of many species. It has also inspired gardeners to seek rarer varieties.

Further knowledge can be gained by joining specialist societies, such as The Hardy Plant Society, which runs a Hardy Geranium Group and there is the Geraniaceae Group of the British Pelargonium and Geranium Society.

ADDENDUM FOR REVISED AND ENLARGED EDITION

Since the first edition of this booklet appeared in 1992 a great many new varieties of geranium have been introduced, particularly hybrids. Although some of these are very similar to existing forms, a number of excellent garden worthy plants are now available. To a great extent we are indebted to Alan Bremner for his dedicated work in raising many outstanding new cultivars, carried out in the inclement weather conditions of Orkney.

Geraniums are still as popular today, possibly even more so, the wide range of varieties providing plants for nearly every situation in the garden.

More nurseries world-wide are specialising in these adaptable plants and *The RHS Plant Finder* is an invaluable source of information for tracking down where to find the plants the gardener is seeking.

Hardiness Zones have not been given for individual geraniums. As well as temperature, factors such as winter wetness affect the survival of a plant, and gardens tend to have different microclimates within them. I find, for instance that *Geranium palmatum* needs protection in my Somerset garden but I have heard of it surviving many cold winters in Leeds. Most hardy geraniums are suited to Zones 6-8, many will be happy in Zones 4-5, a few will tolerate Zone 3. Where a species is more tender this is mentioned in the text.

Gregarious Geraniums

PAT COLLISON

WHENEVER I AM ASKED 'What would look nice with ...?' one or more of the hardy geranium family immediately comes to mind. Versatile, colourful, hard working and attractive in flower and foliage, you can find a geranium for every situation from rock garden to mixed border, from woodland to meadow. This versatility, allied to a colour range of white, pale to deep pinks, mauves and blues, also makes geraniums perfect material for those of us who enjoy colour scheming and plant associations.

June is, traditionally, the month of roses. It is also the month when many of the most colourful geraniums are giving of their best and they make joyful companions. One of the easiest and most widely grown ('common' sounds so rude) is *G.* x *magnificum,* with sheaves of satin sheened violet blue flowers - just right for planting at the foot of a pink or yellow rose, together, perhaps, with *Lamium maculatum* 'Album' (or the silver-leaved *L. m.* 'White Nancy') and *Alchemilla mollis.* The daintier, blue-flowered *G* 'Johnson's Blue' is equally lovely. Or, to increase the cool serenity of a white-flowered rose, plant beside it the geranium 'Mrs Kendall Clark', with beautifully veined light lavender-blue flowers and *Linaria purpurea* 'Canon Went' with slender spires of shell pink, rising above a foreground of grey cotton lavender and *G. sanguineum striatum* (syn. *G. lancastriense*). *G.* 'Mrs Kendall Clark' also looks lovely with the glaucous, ferny foliage and fluffy pale-lemon flowers of *Thalictrum flavum* subsp. *glaucum* (syn. *T. speciosissimum*) and, since their seasons sometimes overlap, it's worth adding a tall bearded iris in pale yellow or blue.

A delicate tracery of veining on the petals is a feature of many geraniums, but in some it is especially attractive. One such is *G. clarkei* 'Kashmir White', whose wide white flowers, poised on thread-like stems above finely cut leaves, have a shading of greyish pink, as though caught in a perpetual twilight of their own. This is a perfect companion for silver foliage, mauve-pink aquilegias, irises and clematis and old roses with cool, grey-washed pink and lavender blooms. The huge starry spheres of *Allium cristophii* and the plump spires of *Penstemon* 'Sour Grapes' also make a nice group with *G.c.* 'Kashmir White'. *G. cinereum* 'Ballerina' with light lavender pink flowers, bewitchingly dark eyed and dark veined, could front the planting, interspersed with purple-leaved *Viola riviniana* Purpurea Group or the black strap-like foliage of *Ophiopogon planiscapus* 'Nigrescens'.

Another geranium with beautifully veined twilight-white flowers is *G. renardii*. This has velvety-soft, grey-green leaves, rounded and lobed and it enjoys sun and good drainage, making it an ideal companion for *Nepeta mussinii* and old cottage pinks growing at the pathside.

Some kind of support is needed for most of the taller growing geraniums, at least while they are in bloom, but some produce long, slender, jointed stems that seem designed to meander gracefully into the lower branches of shrubs. One such is *G.* 'Brookside', whose rich blue, white-eyed flowers are produced through summer and well into autumn: lovely with pink, yellow, white or even orange roses, or the creamy-white and pale green variegated *Cornus alba* 'Elegantissima'. It also looks charming spreading amongst yellow flowered hemerocallis and green leaved yellow edged hostas. *Geranium wallichianum* 'Buxton's Variety' is another beautiful white-eyed blue which acts in a similar fashion, though on a smaller scale, and associates well with variegated mints, or with *Morina longifolia* and white flowered parahebes.

All blue geraniums have a tinge of violet, some more than others, and all the pinks lean towards the blue end of the spectrum (except *G. sanguineum* var. *striatum*). Nevertheless some can sizzle just as hotly as the brightest scarlet - *G. psilostemon* and *G. cinereum* in particular are guaranteed to hold their own in the most flamboyant company. Because of their brilliance, care is needed when choosing neighbours. Silver, whites and blues are safe as well as attractive, but for anyone who can enjoy the barbaric splendour of massed clashing pinks, reds, oranges and magentas, they are totally irresistible. Less violent but still searingly bright, is the combination of magenta and yellow: for instance *G. psilostemon* with tall achilleas or a background of *Weigela* 'Looymansii Aurea' or *Cornus alba* 'Spaethii'. Given a plain evergreen background the magenta and yellow combination can be mellowed considerably by the addition of creamy plumed *Aruncus dioicus* (syn. *A. sylvester*) or the daintier *A.d.* 'Kneiffii' and the green and white striped grass, *Phalaris arundinacea* var. *picta*.

The jazzy brilliance of *G. psilostemon* can be further soothed by planting it with *Lavatera* 'Barnsley', the tall blue-mauve *Nepeta* 'Six Hills Giant', *Salvia nemorosa* 'Ostfriesland' and *Artemisia* 'Lambrook Silver' or 'Powis Castle'. With a background of purple clematis and an edging of lavenders and santolinas and mauve and white violas, this would be a group with which even the most timid of us could relax.

Many of the geraniums make superb ground cover plants, one of the best being *G. macrorrhizum* in its varieties. Of these the rich magenta flowered *G.m.* 'Bevan's Variety' and the similar, *G.m.* 'Czakor' make showy carpets round yellow or white variegated shrubs, the silver *Pyrus salicifolia*

'Pendula', or interspersed with ferns, white flowered foxgloves and white edged *Hosta undulata* var. *marginata* in shade under trees. The pink-flushed, white flowered *G. macrorrhizum* 'Album' looks especially attractive with mahogany leaved shrubs such as *Cotinus coggygria* 'Royal Purple' or *Berberis x ottawensis* f. *purpurea*.

Many geraniums grow equally well in sun or shade and are particularly valuable for their tolerance of dry shade. One such is *G. phaeum*, whose flowers include intriguingly dusky tones of reddish purplish black that beg to be combined with pale foxgloves, lamiums with silver splashed leaves, the white lacy umbels of sweet cicely (or even hedge parsley) and shrubs with yellow or white variegated foliage.

Even when not in flower geraniums make worthy contributions to the garden scene with their maple-like leaves, broadly or finely cut, contrasting nicely with the narrow foliage of ornamental grasses, irises and hemero-callis, the wide leaves of hostas and bergenias, or the silver filigree of artemisias and santolinas. Who, in fairness, could ask for more?

Geranium macrorrhizum

Hardy Geraniums for Foliage Effects
TREVOR BATH

ARDY GERANIUMS are usually spoken of in terms of their flowers, which come in a good range of colours and are often produced for weeks on end. This aspect of the plants has however rather diverted attention from the leaves, which provide many variations on a theme. The basic leaf-shape is a five-pointed one. Sometimes the sections have shallow notches and indentations but more often they are divided and sub-divided into all sorts of pleasingly different patterns. The size, and sometimes the shape, varies between the main, basal leaves, and any leaves borne on the flowering stems. With some of the smaller growing varieties the leaves give a general impression of being more circular than pointed but within that shape the divisions tend to be more intricate and lacy.

There are only a few hardy geranium leaves with variegation but there are infinite gradations of green, sometimes two shades of green on the same leaf. In some varieties the young spring leaves or the old autumn leaves, are distinguished by brilliant colours of red, yellow or cream. Others are noteworthy for attractive spots or blotches or distinctive veining.

There is a suitable hardy geranium for any position in the garden. Here is a representative selection of just a few foliage varieties with particularly interesting details, although every variety has its own interest. They all repay close study, and I do not believe there is a dull leaf among them.

SMALL LEAVED VARIETIES

G. argenteum. Outstanding for its small silvery leaves, a characteristic transmitted to its hybrids with *G. cinereum,* known as *G. x lindavicum,* of which the varieties *G. x l.* 'Apple Blossom' and *G. x l.* 'Lissadell' are particularly attractive. All of these are on such a miniature scale that they really need to be grown in containers, sinks or on scree beds to be fully appreciated.

G. x cantabrigiense This hybrid between *G. macrorrhizum* and *G. dalmaticum* has shiny leaves like a larger version of the latter, with an aromatic quality derived from the former. It makes a compact mat.

G. dalmaticum Small neat shiny leaves that develop a red edge and colour well, especially in the sunny well-drained sites that they prefer.

G. orientalitibeticum (*G. stapfianum* var. *roseum* misapplied) A name which needs constant practice. A low-growing plant with nicely divided leaves in two shades of green and yellow, which dies down at the end of the summer but can increase quite rapidly by the multiplication of its strange, bead-like roots. If allowed some space, an established colony can look delightful as a companion planting with dwarf sedums, for example.

G. renardii I have no hesitation in naming this as my number one favourite. The unique leaves are a soft sage-green, velvety to the touch, with a distinctive scalloped edge. It forms a neat low mound, gradually increasing without becoming invasive. I would even forego the flowers, attractive as they are, for the sheer delight of the leaves.

G. sanguineum Both the species and the named varieties have masses of small, intricately cut leaves and, given a situation in a wall or paving, they will mound up nicely and form a superb foil to the flowers. In the autumn the leaves come into their own, when brilliant colours emphasise and dramatise the filigree shapes so that they look like sprays of burning snow crystals.

G. sessiliflorum subsp. **novae-zelandiae 'Nigricans'** It forms a low-growing, dense clump of small dun-coloured leaves, highlighted by the occasional orange one. A difficult plant to place, since its dull colour needs displaying against a lighter coloured background of gravel or paving for maximum effect. It looks well with other carefully chosen small plants that have contrasting or toning leaves The cultivar 'Porter's Pass' has deep, red leaves, and both forms have been used to create hybrids, notably by Alan Bremner. The size and colour of these vary considerably and often give rise to further spontaneous seedlings in the garden.

MEDIUM-LEAVED VARIETIES.

G. 'Ann Folkard' This hybrid from G. procurrens and G. psilostemon has the trailing habit of the former but without its ability to root as it goes along. The young leaves have a distinct golden flush, well displayed when grown through a shrub or mounded up in paving.

G. 'Blue Sunrise' (G. wallichianum 'Buxton's Variety' x G. 'Ann Folkard') Very similar in habit to 'Ann Folkard' but the young leaves are bright gold and retain their colour though it becomes paler as they mature. However it is still sufficiently distinctive to emphasise the shape of the beautifully fretted leaves, The blue flowers are not to everyone's taste, but I think the combination works very well in this instance.

G. incanum Very finely dissected, greyish leaves on trailing stems that give a very elegant effect. Not entirely hardy but can be kept going by over-wintering cuttings.

G. malviflorum (*G. atlanticum* misapplied) Outstanding for its unusual part-time life style. The finely cut leaves appear in September and provide a useful patch of hardy green foliage all winter. If grown in a sunny well-drained spot they will be joined by spectacular flowers in May, then the whole plant dies down for a summer rest. If grown in a shady situation where it fails to flower I think it is still well worth growing for the sake of the over-wintering foliage alone.

G. nodosum My number two favourite. Very attractive bright green shiny leaves, five-lobed at the base, three-lobed on the flowering stems. Good in shade.

G. robustum Of South African origin but much hardier than might therefore be assumed. In fact, when well suited (it likes gravel) it will seed around nicely. Stylish, finely divided grey-green leaves, more silvery on the reverse.

G. x oxonianum 'Walter's Gift' (*G. x oxonianum x G. versicolor*) The reddish-brown blotches on each lobe are larger and more attractive than on *G. versicolor* itself.

G. wallichianum The typical species is rarely seen, having been displaced by the more fashionable *G.w.* 'Buxton's Variety', but it is by no means to be despised, with its trailing stems of dark green, mottled leaves, which take on brilliant red tones in the winter.

LARGE - LEAVED VARIETIES

G. macrorrhizum The handsome, broadly lobed leaves are a good background for its flowers and are usually evergreen, with reddish tinges in the autumn and winter. They are also highly aromatic. The variegated form is especially desirable, with creamy yellow edgings and overlays on green. It requires more care and attention than the other forms but will light up a semi-shady, dampish location, especially when associated with other plants of distinctive, long-lasting foliage value. The cultivar *G.m.* 'White-Ness' has its own delicate charm, with smaller pale green leaves.

G. maderense The species with the largest, most spectacular foliage. The big, rather ferny, leaves cover a wide area, the leaf stalks eventually leaning their elbows on the ground to support the luxuriant top growth. Originating from Madeira, it needs shelter, preferably under glass in a large greenhouse or in a very large, protected container, to give of its best.

G. x oxonianum 'Claridge Druce. Quickly makes a large clump of dramatic dark-green, spotted leaves. In the right place, a wild garden or woodland planting, it is invaluable, with its striking show of substantial leaves for most of the year. In smaller-scale areas it should be introduced with caution.

G. phaeum 'Variegatum' Splendid edgings and markings of cream and red on a dark green background, very subtle and attractive. Some clones seem to have more constant variegation than others that revert to plain green at the height of the season but a severe haircut will usually produce a good second crop of variegated leaves.

G. platyanthum (syn. *G. eriostemon*) Strongly textured dark green leaves, with a shape reminiscent of hollyhock leaves. Good autumn colour.

G. pratense Large, well-cut leaves , which sometimes suffer from mildew in a dry season, around the time when the flowers are fading: this is another plant that benefits from being cut to the ground at that time, to stimulate fresh new growth. This then acts as a tactful accompaniment to bare-stemmed colchicum flowers, and the new spring growth of the geraniums will in turn help to disguise the decaying colchicum leaves. *G.p.* Midnight Reiter strain is a fairly new and distinguished addition to the roster. It is very variable from seed, but the smallest, slowest-growing seedlings will eventually develop wonderfully dramatic dark leaves, slightly sinister, which are almost black in the best forms.

G. psilostemon The big heraldic leaves associate well with shrubs and tall perennials, and are notable for splendid autumn colour. In addition, the emerging leaf buds and stipules in spring are a brilliant red.

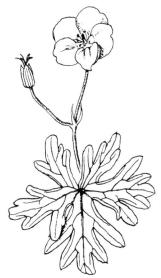

Geranium orientalitibeticum

Geraniums as Ground Cover
JUDITH BRADSHAW

WITH THEIR ATTRACTIVE FOLIAGE and flowers, easy cultivation, propagation and their ability to spread quickly and smother weeds, geraniums must be among the best of ground cover plants. I have grown them for over twenty years in many parts of the garden and by careful selection can have flowers, attractive foliage and easy maintenance from spring to late autumn.

In shade or woodland *G. phaeum* and its cultivars form evergreen clumps, their dainty muted flowers looking lovely from April to June, or even earlier in the south. Especially beautiful is *G.p.* 'Samobor', its heavily marked leaves toning beautifully with maroon flowers. *G.* x *monacense* and *G. reflexum* are just as effective, covering dry ground around conifers in my garden, whilst the pink *G. maculatum* and white *G.m.* f. *albiflorum* form weed-proof cover in damper soil. *G. macrorrhizum* flowers in May; I find *G. m.* 'Czakor' and 'Ingwersen's Variety' give cover in my driest shadiest situations where little else will grow. In these conditions a top dressing of fresh soil and fertiliser every 2-3 years encourages the rhizomes to root and spread. The macrorrhizums grow equally well in sun, where their foliage colours well in autumn; a lovely new cultivar is *G.m.* 'White-Ness'. In May to June *G.* 'Stephanie' has large, veined blue flowers standing well above a strong clump of evergreen felted leaves, whilst a little later *G. sylvaticum* gives early colour in herbaceous borders. *G.s.* 'Mayflower' is still one of the best but we can now choose from a wide range of colours: the soft pink of 'Baker's Pink', pale mauve in 'Cyril's Fancy', the pure white 'Album', through blue ('Amy Doncaster') to the purple of 'Meran'. In well-drained sunny places *G. renardii* slowly spreads its lovely felted foliage, or we can grow instead the similar leaves of *G.* 'Philippe Vapelle' or *G.* 'Chantilly'. In partial shade the rhizomes of *G. clarkei* 'Kashmir White' creep steadily to make a solid patch covered with large white, purple-veined flowers in May-June, whilst in full sun *G.c.* 'Kashmir Purple' smothers a square metre of ground with its glowing flowers. *G.c.* 'Kashmir Pink' is attractive but less vigorous and a new introduction, *G.c.* 'Kashmir Green' (white with green veining) has yet to prove its merits as ground cover. In the same months *G. himalayense* and its cultivars 'Gravetye' and 'Baby Blue' give dense masses of low foliage and large violet-blue flowers. I have the purplish-pink double *G.h.* 'Plenum' but it is much less vigorous; I also find *G.h.* 'Irish Blue' slower to cover.

June heralds the largest flush of geranium flowers. *G. endressii* and its cultivars start blooming in shades of pink and continue until autumn in sun or shade. *G. versicolor* and its white form *G.v.* 'Snow White' prefer shade whilst their hybrid, *G. x oxonianum* in its many shades, from the palest *G. x o.* 'Trevor's White' to the dark pink 'Phoebe Noble', grow equally well in sun or shade. In very dry places I find *G. x o.* 'Claridge Druce' or 'Rose Clair' perform best. In sun *G. asphodeloides* is a good frontal plant whilst further back in the border the tall clumps of *G. pratense* flower in profusion in shades of purple, blue, pink and white during June and into July. The large white flowers of *G.p.* f. *albiflorum* rise to 90cm (3ft). Not quite so vigorous but with the loveliest flowers are *G.p.* 'Plenum Violaceum' and 'Plenum Caeruleum', a stunning sight in June, soon to be followed by a new introduction of ours from Cyril Foster, *G.p.* 'Misty Morn', a blue-grey semi-double of the same height and vigour. For neat edging *G. x cantabrigiense* is excellent in sun; 20cm (8in) high, it gives masses of pink flowers and aromatic semi-evergreen foliage making a weed-proof barrier, whilst Alan Bremner's introduction, 'St Ola', is pure white.

One of the showiest June geraniums is *G. x magnificum* with its four weeks' explosion of colour, good cover for the rest of the season and burnished foliage in autumn. I grow it near the exotic *G. palmatum* with its massive rosette of evergreen leaves smothering a wide area and its pink flowers rising to 90cm (3ft). I have only lost it twice in 15 years in very wet winters and there are always a few self-sown seedlings to replace it. An alternative to *G. x magnificum* is *G.* 'Sirak' with large pink flowers blooming well in sun or part shade. *G. psilostemon*, 90cm (3ft), with its splash of magenta, black centred, flowers and large mounds of attractive leaves is a good choice for the back of a June border. Some excellent hybrids having *G. psilostemon* as one of their parents have been lately introduced; shorter and longer flowering, they are ideal for frontal positions. *G.* 'Nicola', 'Patricia', 'Ivan' and 'Anne Thomson' all have vivid pink flowers in various tones and black eyes; all give good cover and attractive foliage. There are equally effective hybrids in blue and lilac shades: *G.* 'Natalie', 'Brookside' and 'Nimbus' cover attractively at the front of borders whilst further back, the deep blue 'Spinners' is excellent.

In drier sunny areas *G. x riversleaianum* 'Russell Prichard', with its trails of grey-green foliage and magenta flowers, or the silvery pink 'Mavis Simpson' flower from June to the frosts; *G.* 'Little Gem' is studded with bright pink flowers over a dense cushion of foliage; *G.* 'Orkney Pink' spreads out in an attractive mat of coloured leaves and masses of pink flowers whilst the brown leaved hybrids such as *G.* 'Dusky Crûg' or *G.* 'Chocolate Candy' with pale pink flowers give a good contrast. *G.*

sanguineum and its cultivars in shades from white through to deep magenta are effective in frontal positions, raised beds or rockeries in sun or some shade. *G. cinereum* provides smaller cushions in well-drained places whilst carpeters range from the gently spreading *G. dalmaticum* to the more invasive *G. pylzowianum, G. orientalitibeticum,* or *G. kotschyi* var. *charlesii.* I use these at the front of borders among taller plants or on large screes where they smother weeds without being troublesome.

July sees *G.* 'Ann Folkard' throw out her long trailing stems ending with sultry magenta black-eyed flowers; it has no bad habits, unlike one of its parents, *G. procurrens,* which is only safe on large banks or rambling among big shrubs or trees. I grow it near large conifers in very dry soil where its marbled foliage and purple black-centred flowers mask the dying spring bulbs. *G. wlassovianum* is a well-behaved clump-former with purple-pink flowers in late summer and foliage which colours well in autumn. I find *G. nodosum* invaluable for late colour in shade; the purple or lilac cultivars enhance shady places and the recent *G.n.* 'Whiteleaf' with purple, white-edged petals is a beauty.

Finally, one of my favourites and one of the latest to flower is *G. wallichianum* 'Buxton's Variety', with china blue, white-centred flowers or the species in pink; at the front of my borders in sun or shade their lovely flowers and marbled foliage take me well into autumn.

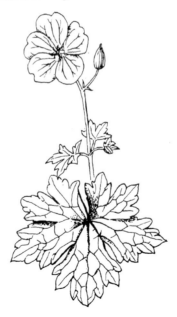

Geranium 'Little Gem'

Cultivation
JOY JONES

MOST GERANIUMS WILL GROW in any reasonable soil in sun or half-shade. Any particular requirements are dealt with in the general list.

PESTS

Aphids: not often troublesome out of doors, but whitefly can be a nuisance in the greenhouse. I dislike using insecticides but in this case it seems to be the most effective way although biological controls (e.g. *Encarsia formosa*) are available.

Slugs and snails: may damage foliage, but they are not usually a serious problem; again, biological controls (nematodes) are available.

Vine weevils: lay their eggs on the soil and the resulting grubs are short, fat and white. They live on the roots, causing foliage to become sickly and wilt. Plants in pots are most at risk, especially in damp, peat-based compost. Suspect plants should be removed and if grubs are found, every scrap of soil washed off the roots with an appropriate insecticide. Replant in fresh soil or compost and clean pots. In the garden, water infested soil with a permitted insecticide picking out and destroying as many grubs as you can find. They are very persistent and may need several doses at intervals. Biological control is also possible.

DISEASES

These are few.

Rust: occasionally affects foliage, which should be removed and destroyed. If badly infected, spray with special rust control fungicide or destroy the plant and start again.

Powdery mildew: occurs mostly in very dry weather. Some forms of *G. pratense* are susceptible. Prevention is better than cure and regular division helps. Cut mildewed foliage to the ground, dust with flowers of sulphur where this is permitted and keep well watered.

Virus: attacks a few species causing distortion of petals. Destroy infected plants and watch seedlings, as the virus can be carried to future generations.

Propagation
REX HARPER

DIVISION OF CLUMPS

With established stocks of geraniums this is by far the easiest way to increase one's plants. It is quite practical to lift a whole clump of a species such as *G. endressii* in the early spring, pull it apart and re-plant sufficient material to make a colourful show during the coming summer. The root divisions can then either be planted out into their flowering positions or potted on to provide stock for exchanges or plant sales.

Most of the vigorous, clump forming species of geraniums can be divided in the above manner but remember to water for a while after re-planting if the weather is dry. Personally I feel that it is not a good idea to divide clumps too early in their lives and I would recommend doing this every third year, rather than on a yearly basis; this applies in particular to the *G. pratense* varieties that always look their best in large, established clumps.

REMOVAL OF SIDE SHOOTS

Spreading species such as *G. macrorrhizum*, *G. clarkei* and *G. dalmaticum* produce many side shoots that can be removed, often with roots attached. These will quickly make new plants and may well flower during the same season if they are planted out in the spring. In the case of the white form of *G. dalmaticum*, which is slow to grow from side shoots and dislikes our wet winters, side shoots are best taken in the autumn and grown on in small pots in a cold frame or greenhouse and planted out in their flowering positions in the spring.

DIVISION OF TUBERS

G. pylzowianum, *G. orientalitibeticum*, *G. malviflorum* and other geraniums which produce tubers can be propagated simply by digging carefully around the main clump and removing small tubers, all of which will grow. Because of the speed with which some of the smaller mountain tuberous–rooted species increase they can present a problem in a rock garden but can be controlled if planted in pots that are sunk into the soil. Many seem to flower better if grown this way; maybe they prefer to be somewhat cramped, as they would be in a mountain crevice.

CUTTINGS

Varieties of geranium that produce long, trailing, but non-rooting stems such as *G.* 'Ann Folkard' and *G. wallichianum* can, in my experience, usually be grown from stem cuttings taken early in the growing season. The cuttings should comprise a node with about one and half centimetres (half an inch) of stem on either side. Remove all but one leaf from the cutting and plant in shallow pots in a mixture of John Innes No. 2 and sharp sand, making sure that the soil is moistened and well firmed down before the cuttings are inserted. The cuttings are then planted flat, covering the stem with soil and allowing just the top of the node to protrude above the soil. Place the pots of cuttings in a cold frame or greenhouse and remember not to let them dry out. Pot on the young plants after they have made reasonable growth.

Some of the clump-forming mountain geraniums, such as *G. cinereum* and its many varieties will eventually make quite woody stems and these provide cuttings which can be obtained with the help of a sharp blade by cutting small sections, each with two or three small leaves at the top, from the parent plant. These cuttings can be taken throughout the growing season and are best planted in pots of well-firmed John Innes No. 2 allowing the cutting to make its own hole in the compost and firming it in with the fingers, just below the leaves. Grow on in a cold frame or greenhouse.

SEED

Growing geraniums from seed can be a fascinating way of propagating your stock if you are prepared to wait a while for the plants to bloom. Although some species like the *G. endressii* and *G. pratense* varieties will give plenty of flowers in the first year from seed, others take at least twelve months to get established before they even think of producing blooms.

Most species seem to germinate well if the seed is sown in a gritty soil compost. John Innes No. 2 with added grit makes a good medium. Water the compost well before sowing the seed thinly on the surface, cover with a dusting of sifted soil and place a sheet of glass over the tray or pot (remembering to leave an air space between the glass and the pot). Keep paper over the glass until the seeds start to germinate, at which time remove both paper and glass and place the trays or pots in a light place in the greenhouse or frame, to encourage growth.

Seedlings can be potted when the second pair of leaves are well developed and can then be grown on in pots until established. Remember to label each pot carefully, as it is all too easy to get varieties mixed up.

Before planting out the seedlings in the garden read up on the varieties that you have grown and find out how each particular geranium would prefer to grow in the wild, then try to copy the type of habitat in your garden. A lot of disappointment can be overcome by taking a little care in positioning plants and not just putting them in odd corners in the hope that they will grow.

Sometimes germination may be prolonged and often one finds

seedlings coming up in pots that contain old compost that has been re-used, which can be most confusing. Therefore give your seeds plenty of time to get going before you give up and empty out the pots. Sometimes placing the pots on a shelf in the greenhouse fairly near the glass seems to help, but don't forget to water them.

Geranium 'Philippe Vapelle'

List of Geraniums in Cultivation
JOY JONES

THE FOLLOWING LIST includes only those geraniums known to be in cultivation, but by no means all. A few will be difficult to track down, though fortunately there are now several excellent nurseries specialising in hardy geraniums. It is also worth while searching through seed lists.

The name of the species is followed by: other names under which it may be found; RHS award; its parentage if a hybrid; places of origin; approximate height (which will obviously vary according to soil and situation) and flowering time (again variable). Flower size refers to the approximate diameter.

SYMBOLS
Prop = propagation, C = cuttings, RC = root cuttings, D = division, S = seed and T = tubers.
* = easy geraniums for beginners
AGM = Award of Garden Merit

G. albanum SE Caucasus and adjacent parts of Iran. 30-45cm (12-18in). June onwards.
Forms substantial clumps of evergreen kidney-shaped, divided leaves from compact rootstock. Flowers approx. 2cm (¾-1in) on long thin, trailing stems, rather chilly pink with magenta veins and slightly notched petals. Rather untidy in habit but useful for its long flowering period in woodland, wild garden or shrub border, where it will weave through neighbouring branches.
Prop: D or S

G. albiflorum N. & C. Asia, NE European Russia. 30cm (12in) May onwards. A low growing, modest but charming plant with deeply divided leaves; stems, leaf margins and sepals purplish brown. Flowers, small, funnel-shaped, white or palest lilac, violet veined, notched petals produced spasmodically over a long period. Prefers light shade.
Prop: D or S

G. anemonifolium see *G. palmatum*

G. 'Ann Folkard' AGM (*G. procurrens* x *G. psilostemon*) An almost sterile hybrid raised by Revd Oliver Folkard in Lincolnshire (1973). An outstanding, much sought-after plant, producing a mass of golden-tinted foliage in spring from a comparatively small crown, later turning green.

Very long, thin non-rooting stems, cover a wide area, scrambling through other plants. Flowers approx. 4cm (1½-1¾in) sumptuous rich purple, shot with pink, black centre and veins. Seems to change colour according to the light. Non-stop flowering from July to autumn.
Prop: D (in spring - care needed) or RC

G. 'Anne Thomson' ★ (*G. traversii* x *G. procurrens*) 60 x 90 cm (2 x 3ft). June-October.
Raised by Alan Bremner from the same parentage as *G.* 'Ann Folkard' but is a more upright, compact plant with copious flowers massed above the foliage. Border in sun.
Prop: D

G. 'Apple Blossom' see *G.* x *lindavicum*

G. argenteum French Alps, Italy, the former Yugoslavia. 10-15cm (4-6in). July-August.
A choice species for the rock garden, scree, trough or alpine house. Neat rosettes of small rounded, divided leaves covered with silvery silky hairs. Flowers 2.5cm (1in), white or pale pink with darker veins and slightly notched petals. Gritty soil in full sun, needing protection from winter wet.
Prop: D or C (with care), RC or S (may not come true)

G. argenteum x **G. cinereum** see *G.* x *lindavicum*

G. aristatum Mountains of S. Albania, S. of the former Yugoslavia, NW Greece. 45cm (18in). June-August.
A distinctive hairy plant, forming hummocks of greyish-green leaves. Flowers 2.5cm (1in) nodding, petals strongly reflexed, white or pale lilac, attractively veined with violet. Reliable and worthy of a place in the border. Sun or part shade.
Prop: D or S (seed may be difficult to germinate: Dr Yeo suggests chipping seeds before sowing)

G. asphodeloides ★ S. Europe. 30-45cm (12-18in). June onwards.
Somewhat variable, makes substantial mounds of fresh-looking, evergreen rounded leaves for wild garden, banks, walls. Sun or shade.

G. asphodeloides subsp. **asphodeloides**
Starry flowers 2.5 cm (1in) pale to deep mauvish-pink, strongly veined with reddish purple. Rather gappy petals. There is also a white form.

G. asphodeloides subsp. **crenophilum**
Flowers rose pink with broad petals.

G. asphodeloides subsp. **sintenisii**
A very free-flowering plant with flowers a pale pink or purple.

G. 'Aya' (*G. traversii* x *G. procurrens*) 7-10cm (3-4in) spreading. June-September.
Raised by Allan Robinson at Wisley Gardens and named after the Japanese girl who found the seedling when working there. Intermediate between its parents, 'Aya' forms close mats of small, rounded leaves studded with tiny deep pink flowers 1½cm (½in) heavily veined with reddish-purple and very dark at the centre. Excellent ground cover, even in dry shade. Not readily available as yet.

G. 'Bertie Crûg' (*G.endressii* x *G. papuana*) 5cm (2in) spreading.
A seedling found in the nursery at Crûg Farm plants and named after the nursery terrier! This diminutive creeper develops mats of shiny bronze leaves and small purplish-pink flowers over a long period. Said to be hardy but not long-lived in my frost-pocket garden. It needs good drainage in rock garden or scree.
Prop: C

G. 'Black Ice' (*G. traversii* var. *elegans* x *sessiliflorum* subsp. *novae-zelandiae* 'Nigricans') Spreading 1m (39in) May-September.
Raised by Alan Bremner. It forms large neat mounds of dark bronze foliage from which radiate long stems carrying small white, occasionally blush-pink flowers. Best grown on a light background of gravel or paving to contrast with the dark leaves.
Prop: C

G. 'Blue Sunrise' (*G. wallichianum* 'Buxton's Variety' x *G.* 'Ann Folkard')
Raised by Hans Kramer in Holland, this offspring has inherited the best of both parents. With the golden foliage of 'Ann Folkard' but longer-lasting, and deep blue flowers larger than 'Buxton's Variety' all summer long; what more could be asked for? Border, sun or part shade.
Prop: D

G. 'Brookside' (probably *G. pratense* x *G. clarkei*) 60cm (2ft). June-August.
A recently introduced hybrid, making clumps of finely cut foliage on reddish stems. Flowers large bowl-shaped of excellent deep blue, white at the centre. A lovely plant for sun or part shade.
Prop: D

G. brutium [annual] Italy, Sicily, Balkan Peninsular, Turkey. 30cm (1ft).
A charmingly small annual plant with mounded light-green, rounded leaves and a profusion of small bright bluish-pink flowers enhanced by bluish black anthers. It self-seeds moderately, especially in gravel and between cracks in paving. Sun or shade.
Prop: S

G. caffrum South Africa. 60cm (2ft). Summer.

Grows from thick taproot; stems slender, woody at the base. Leaves very deeply cut with narrow lobes and sharply toothed. Flowers small but prolific, usually white, sometimes pink with shallowly notched petals. Reasonably hardy in light soil.

Prop: C or S (self sows quite freely)

G. canariense Canary Islands. 60cm (2ft). Spring onwards.

Basal rosette of handsome, deeply divided large aromatic leaves, growing from a stem a few inches above the soil. Leaf stalks flushed brownish purple. Numerous flowers 4cm (1½in) deep pink, rather widely spaced petals, pale on the underside, nearly white or dark at the base. Not fully hardy and short-lived (up to three years). Greenhouse or warm sheltered corner in well-drained soil in milder areas.

Prop: S

G. x cantabrigiense (*G. dalmaticum* x *G. macrorrhizum*) 30cm (1ft). June-July.

Cheerful, compact mats of glossy, aromatic, evergreen foliage, spreading steadily, but not rampantly. Flowers 2.5cm (1in) bright pink, abundantly produced. Leaves and flowers midway between parents. *G. x c.* 'Biokovo' is less compact and not so vigorous with white, slightly pink-tinged flowers. Both good ground cover, front of the border, large rock garden in sun or part shade.

Prop: D (sterile)

G. 'Carol' A *G. cinereum* cultivar of unknown parentage. 15cm (6in). June-September.

A recent introduction from Carl and Janet Lowe in Shropshire. Large bright cerise flowers, distinctly veined with reddish purple and with a dark eye, are held over a low clump of *G. cinereum* type foliage. It is very free flowering over a long period. Rock garden, trough or scree in sun and well-drained soil.

Prop: C

G. cataractarum S. Spain, Morocco. 30cm (1ft). June onwards.

A pretty plant with aromatic deeply divided ferny leaves:: evergreen. Flowers 2cm (¾in), funnel-shaped, bright pink with orange-red anthers. Rock garden or trough in half shade. Moderately hardy, though not very long-lived.

Prop: S

G. 'Chantilly' (*G. gracile* x *G. renardii*) 45cm (18in). May-August

Raised by Alan Bremner and introduced by Axletree Nursery. An upright plant bearing clouds of luminous lavender-pink flowers with separated

notched petals, lightly veined, borne well above the light green wrinkled and hairy leaves. Seems to prefer some shade that is not too dry.
Prop: D

Geranium 'Carol'

G. 'Chocolate Candy' 22cm (9in) June-September.
A one-off seedling that appeared when Coen Jansen (Vaste Planten, Holland) was trialing seedlings from *G.* 'Stanhoe (*G. sessiliflorum* x *G. traversii*). Forms mounds of luscious dark chocolate foliage topped with small pale pink flowers. Unfortunately it is not fully hardy, needing sharp drainage in full sun and winter protection in cold damp areas. Sadly, I lost mine.
Prop: C

G. cinereum Central Pyrenees. 15cm (6in). June onwards.
Neat rosettes of small, rounded, divided leaves of greyish green. Flowers 4cm (1½in) on lax stems, white or pink, finely pencilled with darker veins. There is a pure white form. Rock garden, scree or trough. Gritty soil in sun.
Prop: D or S (seedlings may vary if other forms grown)

G.c. 'Ballerina' AGM ⋆ Flowers 3cm (1¼in) purplish pink, petals notched, covered with a strong network of dark veins and dark blotch at the base. Most attractive and reliable. Raised by Blooms of Bressingham.
Prop: D or C

G.c. 'Lawrence Flatman' ⋆ Another winner from Blooms, similar to *G.c.* 'Ballerina' but with dark blotches near the top of the petals.

G. cinereum var. *subcaulescens* AGM Balkan Peninsula, C. & NE Turkey. 22cm (9in). May onwards.
Low-growing mounds of small, rounded, dark green leaves. Flowers 2.5cm (1in) fierce magenta, very dark centre and dark veins, black anthers. Rock garden but keep well away from red-flowered plants! *G.c.* var *s.* 'Giuseppii' has rather more silvery leaves, near-magenta flowers with less pronounced central area. *G.c.* var. *s.* 'Splendens' flowers less strident in colour, dark centre, nicely veined.
Prop: D or C

G. 'Claridge Druce' see *G.* x *oxonianum*

G. clarkei Kashmir 45cm (18in). June onwards.
Two cultivars generally grown, both spreading by underground rhizomes producing finely cut, feathery leaves. Sun or part-shade.

G.c. 'Kashmir Green' A new introduction from Coen Jansen of Vaste Plantern in Holland. It sounds very desirable but is not yet readily available. Taller than other forms of *G. clarkei* at50cm (20in), it has white flowers with green veins merging to a green centre. The leaves are finely cut, suggesting some relationship with *G. pratense.*

G.c. 'Kashmir Purple' ⋆ (syn. *G. pratense* 'Kashmir Purple') *G. bergianum* misapplied. Spreads rapidly and can be invasive. Good groundcover for large areas. Flowers 4cm (1½in), facing upwards, deep violet purple, red veins.
Prop: D or S

G.c. 'Kashmir White' AGM ⋆ *G. rectum* 'Album' misapplied. A beautiful plant, less vigorous than its purple counterpart. Flowers 4cm (1½-1¾in), white with delicate lilac-pink veins, giving a mauvish-grey flush to the petals.
Prop: D or S (some seedlings may revert to purple)

G. collinum * SE Europe, C. & E. Turkey, W. & C. Asia. 45-60cm (18-24in). All summer.
Bushy clumps of deeply divided and finely cut grey-green leaves, sometimes primrose yellow tinged with pink in spring Flowers 3cm (1-1½in), saucer-shaped, usually mid-pink, but can be lighter or darker. Useful in the border for its long flowering period and resistance to drought conditions.
Prop: D or S

G. 'Coombland White' (*G. lambertii* x *G. traversii* var. *elegans*). 30cm (1ft), spreading.
Raised by the late Rosemary Lee of Coombland Nursery. This beautiful plant makes large hummocks of rounded mottled leaves with long trailing stems. The exquisite flowers are comparable to those of *G. lambertii* 'Swansdown': white with lilac veins converging to a dark violet centre. Grow in full sun and well-drained soil and allow plenty of space. Large rock garden, gravel garden or scree. May need winter protection in cold, wet soil.
Prop: C

G. 'Cyril's Fancy' (*G. sylvaticum* x *G. albiflorum*). 30 x 90cm (1 x 3ft). July-October.
Raised by Cyril Foster, Rothbury. A robust plant resembling *G. sylvaticum* with large leaves and distinct large, pale lilac flowers with widely spaced petals produced in profusion. Border in sun or part shade, where not too dry.
Prop: D

G. dahuricum NE Asia, W. China. 45cm (18in). June-August.
A sprawler with thin lax stems, small finely cut leaves with narrow, rather widely spaced lobes. New leaves emerging in spring are delicate pink and cream. Flowers 3cm (1¼in), saucer-shaped pale pink with dark red veins. Large rock garden or wild garden in full sun.
Prop: D or S

G. dalmaticum AGM SW of the former Yugoslavia, Albania. 10-15cm (4-6in). June-July.
Dwarf, slowly spreading, neat hummocks of small, evergreen, aromatic shiny leaves. Flowers 2cm (¾in), lovely shell pink, held well above the foliage. Needs frequent division. Rock garden, trough or paving in sun. Good autumn tints.
Prop: D or RC

G. dalmaticum 'Album' A desirable white form, though less vigorous.

G. 'Derrick Cook' Collected by Derrick Cook in 1978 above the tree line near Naran Nag in Kashmir and considered by Peter Yeo to be a very interesting form of *G. himalayense*. The flowers are impressively large, 5cm

(2in) or more, occasionally produced in pairs on the same stem. Similar to *G. clarkei* 'Kashmir White' in colour but with more pronounced, darker veins and overlapping petals forming a rounder flower. When well grown the leaves are very large. Quite hardy, grows well in most situations but flowering at its best in full sun. This exceptionally beautiful geranium should be available early in 2001.
Prop: D (sets very few seeds)

G. 'Dilys' (*G. sanguineum* x *G. procurrens*). 23 x 90cm (9 x 36in). July-October.
Raised by Alan Bremner and introduced by Axletree Nursery; named after Dilys Davies. The foliage, very similar to *G. sanguineum*, is produced on long thin trailing stems (non-rooting), with reddish-purple, dark-eyed flowers. Valuable for its long flowering season, even into December during mild spells. Large rock garden or front of the border, weaving through other plants or shrubs.
Prop: D

G. donianum Himalayas, SW China, Tibet. 15-45cm (6-18in).
Kidney-shaped, deeply divided, marbled leaves from thick rootstock. Flowers funnel-shaped, upwardly inclined, reddish purple. Not very long-lived but easily raised from seed. Rather lost in the flower border, best in rock garden.
Prop: S

G. 'Elworthy Dusky' 30cm (1ft). May-July.
A delightful geranium found growing in the nursery of Elworthy Garden Plants (Jenny Spiller); probably a seedling from *G.* 'Brookside'. The substantial clumps bear ethereal clouds of off-beat dusky pink flowers that are very charming. Border in sun.
Prop: D

G. endressii * S. Europe, W. Asia. 45cm (18in). June-September.
Leafy clumps of almost evergreen, light green, divided and attractively pointed leaves, providing dense colonising ground cover. Flowers 3cm (1-1½in), funnel-shaped, bright chalky pink with notched petals, over a very long period. Cut to the ground towards end of July, when becoming untidy, to produce fresh growth and flowers. Front of the border, light woodland, under shrubs, especially old roses.
Prop: D or S (may not come true)

G. endressii x **G. versicolor** see *G.* x *oxonianum*

G. erianthum E. Siberia, Japan, Alaska, Canada (N. British Columbia). 45-60cm (18-24in). May-June and later. Resembles *G. platyanthum* (syn. *G. eriostemon*) but leaves more deeply divided; divisions overlapping with

numerous sharply pointed lobes and teeth. Good autumn colour. Flowers 4cm (1½in), flattish, varying from pale to rich violet blue and darkly veined. A plant of great charm for border, light woodland and beneath shrubs in sun or part shade.
Prop: D or S

G.e. **'Calm Sea'** Taller than the type, with beautiful soft-grey-blue flowers strikingly marked with dark feathered veins.

G.e. **'Neptune'** Has larger, deeper blue flowers.

G.e. **'Undine'** A shorter version with pure white flowers.

G. eriostemon see *G. platyanthum*

G. farreri AGM W. China. 10-15cm (4-6in). May-June.
Introduced by Farrer in 1917. A gem for the rock garden, scree, trough or alpine house. Small, rounded, divided leaves, reddish margins and stems. Flowers 3cm (1-1½in) exquisite soft pink and conspicuous, bluish-black anthers. Well drained, light sandy/gritty soil in full sun.
Prop: D (by careful division of crowns with tap-root attached) or S

G. fremontii Western N. America. 30-45cm (12-18in). June-September.
A distinctive, sticky hairy geranium with numerous deeply divided leaves, coarsely lobed and toothed. Flowering stems much branched and leafy. Flowers 4cm (1½in), flat, upward facing, pale to deep pink, petals usually notched. Needs frequent re-planting as roots tend to become exposed. Rather too large and untidy for the average rock garden, though useful for its long flowering period in a sunny border. Self-sown seedlings occur occasionally.
Prop: D or S

G. gracile NE Turkey, Caucasus. 45-60cm (18-24in). All summer.
Resembles *G. nodosum* but taller and hairier. Leaves light green, wrinkled with diamond-shaped divisions. Flowers funnel-shaped delicate pink, enhanced by fascinating short 'eyelash' veins. A graceful plant indeed for woodland or shady corners.
Prop: D or S

G. gymnocaulon NE Turkey, SW Caucasus. 30-45cm (12-18in). July-August.
Allied to *G. ibericum* but less vigorous and later flowering. Flowers 4cm (1½in), rich violet blue with darker veins and notched petals. Tends to be rather short-lived. Large rock garden or borders.
Prop: D or S

G. harveyi R.S.A., Transkei - Cape 10cm (4in).
Grows in mountains at 1300-2000m in rocky ground, forming a cascade of

attractive deeply cut and toothed silvery leaves 3cm (1in), silkily hairy on woody stems. Small magenta-pink flowers are only occasionally produced. An eye-catching sight when planted to trail through rocks. Hardy in Somerset at the bottom of a valley in a frost pocket over the past four years. Prop: C. Seed very sparse

G. hayatanum B&SWJ 164 Asia – Formosa, Korea in mountains at 4300m. Collected by Bleddyn Wynn-Jones in Taiwan. An interesting species with velvety light green marbled foliage, darkening with age and assuming deep brownish-black blotches. Small, 3cm (1½in) puce pink white-eyed flowers with darker veins are carried on sturdy, red trailing stems. Large rock garden, raised bed in sun or part shade. Prop: S

G. himalayense ⋆ (syns *G. grandiflorum* and *G. meeboldii*) Himalayas. 30-45cm (12-18in). June. Excellent weed smothering, spreading ground cover. Handsome finely cut leaves taking on brilliant autumn tints. Flowers 5cm (2in), saucer-shaped, violet blue flushed reddish pink, produced spasmodically after main flowering until autumn. Needs space to spread under trees or shrubs. Lovely with yellows, pinks and purples. Prop: D

G.h. 'Baby Blue' 30cm (1ft). April-July. A compact form with extra large flowers of a beautiful blue – very appealing!

G.h. 'Gravetye' AGM Somewhat shorter with smaller leaves and larger flowers, the reddish central zone being more pronounced.

G.h. 'Irish Blue' Introduced from Eire by Mr Graham Thomas; flowers are a beautiful pale blue, with even larger central zone. Hardly ever without flowers from June to October.

G.h. 'Plenum' (syn. *G.h.* 'Birch Double') Small rounded leaves; flowers 2.5cm (1in) soft lilac blue, fully double, flushed with pink. A charming little plant 25cm (10in), not very vigorous, sun or part shade, where not too dry. Prop: D (sterile)

G. ibericum subsp. **ibericum** NE Turkey, Caucasus. 45cm (18in). June. Handsomely divided leaves with divisions overlapping; numerous lobes and teeth. Flowers approx 5cm (1½ to 2in) deep violet with darker, feathered veins and notched petals. Flowering period rather short but often produces a few blooms in autumn. Border or under shrubs in sun. Prop: D or S

G.i. subsp. ***jubatum*** **'White Zigana'** 50cm (20in).

Collected by Michael Baron in the Zigana Pass, NE Turkey. Similar to the blue flowered plant but with white, purple-veined blooms 4cm (1½in). Not yet readily available but definitely one to look out for.
Prop: D

G. incanum var. ***multifidum*** South Africa. 20cm (8in). All summer. Forms low tussocks of very finely cut feathery leaves, dark green above, silvery beneath. Flowers 2.5cm (1in), deep reddish purple with darker veins, white at centre. Good trailing over edge of troughs or sprawling over rocks in sun. Not reliably hardy.
Prop: C (need protection in winter) S (self-sown seedlings sometimes appear)

G. 'Ivan' (*G. psilostemon* x *G. oxonianum*) 60cm (2ft). June- September.
Named after Ivan Lovette, Belgium. This is a real stunner, developing big clumps of handsome leaves resembling those of *G. psilostemon*. The flowers are also similar but more rounded with slightly overlapping petals and concentrated in a great mass, just above the foliage.
Prop: D

G. 'Johnson's Blue' AGM ⋆ (*G. himalayense* x *G. pratense*) 30-45cm (12-18in). June onwards.
Leafy, spreading clumps of elegant, finely cut foliage, providing dense ground cover - a strong grower. Flowers 5cm (2in), good lavender blue, tinged pink at centre, fluttering well above the foliage.
Prop: D (sterile)

G. 'Joy' (*G. traversii* var. *elegans* x *G. lambertii*) 30cm (1ft). June-September.
Raise by Alan Bremner, named after the writer, and introduced by Axletree Nursery. 'Joy' makes quite a substantial mound of evergreen marbled leaves. The cup-shaped flowers, produced on trailing stems, are a very pretty pale pink with a silky sheen and reddish-purple veins. Large rock garden or front of border in well-drained soil.
Prop: D or C in spring

G. 'Kashmir Blue' (*G. clarkei* 'Kashmir White x *G. pratense* f. *albiflorum*) 60cm (2ft). June-August.
Raised by Ivan Lovette in Belgium. Similar to *G. pratense* in size and habit with appealing soft, violet-blue flowers; a good companion for magenta flowered geraniums.
Prop: D

G. 'Kate' (syn. *G. 'Kate Folkard'*), (*G. endressii* x *G. sessiliflorum*) 10-15cm (4-6in). June onwards

This hybrid appeared in the garden of Revd Oliver Folkard in Lincolnshire and is named after his daughter. A delightful dwarf plant with small, rounded, cut leaves of bronzy green similar to those of *G. sessiliflorum* 'Nigricans'. Sepals also tinged with brown. Flowers 1.5cm (½-¾in), funnel-shaped, pale pink with dark veins on thin trailing stems. Rock garden, scree, trough or alpine house. Tends to die out and may need winter protection.

Prop: D (sterile)

Geranium 'Joy'

G. 'Khan' (*G. sanguineum* x *G. wlassovianum?*) 40cm (16in) June-August. A recent introduction from Wisley Gardens in Surrey, resembling *G. sanguineum*, though much larger in leaf, flower and height. Flowers, 5cm (2in), produced in abundance are a clear bright magenta-purple and create a dazzling display, especially amongst white-flowered plants.

Prop: D

G. kishtvariense Kashmir. 30cm (1ft). All summer.
A recent introduction by Roy Lancaster (1978). A bushy plant, creeping by underground stolons. Leaves deeply divided with few broad lobes, bright green and wrinkled. Flowers 4cm (1½in), facing upwards on thin stems,

rich pinkish-purple, white at centre and finely veined. Prefers some shade. Woodland or shady corner.
Prop: D or S

G. koreanum Asia – Korea mountain woodland areas near streams.
This choice species is rather like G. *hayatanum* in habit, with nicely marbled deeply toothed leaves on trailing stems, colouring well in autumn. Large flowers, 4cm (1½in), with separated petals are a lovely shade of rose-pink with deeper veins and pale at the centre. Large rock garden, front of border, preferring some moisture.
Prop: S

G. krameri N. China, CIS, Korea, Japan. July-September.
Distinctive leaves, very deeply cut with narrow coarsely serrated lobes. Flowers 3cm (1-1¼in). flat, rose pink with darker veins on long trailing thin, rather lax, stems. Prefers shade in woodland or wild garden. Interesting but no real garden value.
Prop: S

G. lambertii (syn. G. *grevilleanum*) Himalayas. 30-45cm (12-18in). Late summer.
Trailing plant with few basal leaves. Leaves wrinkled with sharply pointed lobes. Flowers 3cm (1-1¼), nodding, saucer-shaped, very delicate pale pink with crimson veining converging into central crimson stain. Strikingly beautiful, though sometimes reluctant to flower. Best scrambling through other plants or shrubs in partial shade.
Prop: S

G.l. 'Swansdown' The exquisite white flowered form: the flowers flushed pink with crimson centres and very pale veins. Leaves mottled with two shades of green.
Prop: S (which comes true)

G. libani (syn. G. *libanoticum*) Lebanon, W. Syria, C. & S. Turkey. 40cm (15in). April-May.
An unusual geranium, leaves shiny dark green with pale veins; rather widely spaced divisions. Flowers 4cm (1½in) violet blue, notched petals and feathery veins. Dormant after flowering, until autumn. The thick roots tend to lie on the surface of the soil and benefit from a mulch, especially in drought conditions. A charmer for the large rock garden, or near front of the border where later flowering plants can fill the gap.
Prop:D or S

G. x lindavicum (G. *argenteum* x G. *cinereum*)

G. x l. 'Alanah' Described by the late Walter Ingwersen (1946) as "a very attractive plant, but slightly less silvery in foliage than *G. argenteum* and extremely free in the production of its vivid crimson-purple flowers. It is shy to increase". He considered it to be the same plant as *G. argenteum purpureum*.

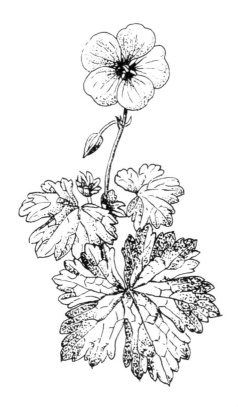

Geranium lambertii 'Swansdown'

G. x l. 'Apple Blossom' (syn. *G. x l.* 'Jenny Bloom')
From Blooms of Bressingham. Neat clumps 15cm (6in) of small, deeply cut, silvery leaves. Flowers (June-August) palest pink, lightly veined - delightful! Rock garden, scree, trough or alpine house in well-drained gritty soil. Protect from winter wet.

G. x l. 'Lissadell' (syn. *G. x l.* 'Lissadell Purple') Compact hummocks of small silvery-green foliage topped by deep plum-coloured flowers - most attractive. Lived for twelve years in a trough in Surrey.
Prop: C or RC (not easy)

G. **'Little Gem'** (*G. oxonianum* x *G.traversii*) 15-20cm (6-8in). June-September.

Raised by Alan Bremner and introduced by Axletree Nursery. This little gem is similar to 'Russell Prichard' but is more compact in habit, making neat mounds of flattish leaves. After a shower of rain the vibrant purple flowers sparkle like small jewels. Regrettably not fully hardy, it needs very well drained soil in full sun and, in cold wet conditions, winter protection. Large rock garden, raised bed, or front of border.
Prop: D

G. lucidum [annual] Europe, Africa, SW & C. China. 30cm (1ft). Spring-summer.

The shining cranesbill. Delightful, but very free with offspring As these are usually confined around the parent plant it makes pretty ground cover for inhospitable dry areas under trees or shrubs. Rosettes of small rounded, succulent leaves on red stems, building up to 30cm (1ft), but usually less in poor soil. Flowers 1cm (½in) deep pink. Some rosettes will be present in winter if germination has taken place in autumn.

G. macrorrhizum * S. Europe. 30-45cm (12-l8in). May-June.

Reliable ground cover, spreading by underground rhizomes. Copious foliage, almost evergreen. Leaves divided, rounded, sticky and aromatic. Good autumn colour. Flowers 2.5cm (1in), dull magenta, reddish bladder-like calyx. A strong grower, but not too rampant. Sun or shade.
Prop: D

G.m. **'Album'** AGM Lovely white-flowered form with faint pink flush.

G. m. **'Bevan's Variety'** Good deep magenta flowers, rather spoilt by red sepals.

G.m. **'Czakor'** Flowers deep magenta pink, an improvement on 'Bevan's Variety'.

G.m. **'Ingwersen's Variety'** AGM One of the prettiest cultivars with soft pink flowers and paler leaves.

G.m. **'Lohfelden'** A small form. 15cm (6in), raised by Hans Klose in Germany. Foliage similar to *G.* x *cantabrigiense* and blush-white flowers strongly veined with deep pink.

G.m. **'Pindus'** Collected by A.W.A. Baker in the Pindus Mountains of N Greece. This dwarf, 20cm (8in) plant, has bright magenta-pink flowers.

G.m. **'Ridsko'** has smooth shiny leaves that are deciduous, magenta-pink flowers and rather sinister looking black rhizomes.

G.m. 'Spessart' A white flowered seedling collected from the wild by Dr Hans Simon. Identical to *G.m.* 'Album' with dark pink calyx and anthers.

G.m. 'Variegatum' Greyish-green leaves splashed with cream. Purplish-pink flowers. Not so vigorous as any of the above, needing regular feeding and some sun. Hopefully someone will raise a white flowered form.

G.m. 'Velebit' Collected by Dr Hans Simon in Croatia. It has reddish-purple narrow, separated petals.

G.m. 'White-Ness' From seed collected by Paul Matthews (Ness Botanic Garden) on Mount Olympus, Greece. Distinct from *G.m.* 'Album', bearing pure white flowers with green calyx and light green foliage. Sometimes sold, wrongly, as 'Mount Olympus'

G. macrostylum Greece, Albania, S. of the former Yugoslavia, C. & W. Turkey. 22cm (9in). May-June.
A pretty plant, spreading rapidly by small tubers. Leaves small and finely cut, dying down after flowering until autumn. Flowers 2.5cm (1in), rather frail, mauvish pink with darker veins and centre. There are also lavender-blue forms, net veined but not dark at the centre. Can be a nuisance in the rock garden; best confined to paving or grown in containers.
Prop: T

G. maculatum NE America. 60-75cm (24-30in). May-July.
Erect plant from strong rootstock. Handsomely fingered, shiny leaves. Flowers 2.5cm (1in), shallow bowl-shaped in clusters, usually pale lilac pink, but can be deeper. Petals notched, white at base. Prefers moist soil in border, streamside or wild garden in sun or part shade.
Prop: D or S

G.m. f. albiflorum A desirable white form, more difficult to cultivate.

G.m. 'Chatto' 40-50cm (16-20in) May-June.
Raised at Beth Chatto's nursery in Essex. This sturdy plant has big, handsome, fingered leaves topped by sprays of large clear pink luminous flowers.

G. maderense AGM Madeira. 1.0-1.2m (3-4ft). February-March onwards.
A magnificent, architectural giant, growing from an impressive rosette of very large, much divided leaves on brownish-red stems. Flowers 4cm (1½in), massed well above the foliage, purplish pink with pale netted veins, dark crimson centre and dark red anthers. Makes a wonderful pot plant, needing winter protection in a greenhouse. May behave as a biennial, dying after flowering, but sometimes grows on from side shoots. Initial growth is rapid and young plants need frequent potting-on, so as not to check their progress.
Prop: S (after storing for a month or two)

G. x *magnificum* AGM * (*G. ibericum* x *G. platypetalum*) 60cm (2ft). June. A vigorous hybrid, superior to both parents. Leaves nearer to *G. platypetalum*, colouring well in autumn. Flowers 5cm (2in), saucer-shaped, rich violet, darkly veined and produced in abundance, magnificent in its few weeks of glory. Excellent ground cover under shrubs in sun or half shade. Lovely with *Iris pallida*, blue grasses and yellow roses.
Prop: D (sterile)

G. malviflorum *G. atlanticum* misapplied. S. Spain, Morocco, Algeria. 22-30cm (9-12in). March-April.
A tuberous rooted geranium. Leaves prettily rounded and finely cut. Flowers 4cm (1½in), violet blue with reddish veins, giving a shot-silk appearance. Poor soil in sun.
Prop: T

G. **'Mavis Simpson'** see *G.* x *riversleaianum*

G. x *monacense* (*G. phaeum* x *G. reflexum*) Good ground cover with characteristics midway between both parents. Leaves usually blotched with brown. Flowers with strongly reflexed dull mauvish purple with central white and violet zone.

G. x *monacense* var. *anglicum* (*G. phaeum* var. *lividum* x *G. reflexum*)
Flowers pale lilac pink, small white central area with wider violet zone, strongly veined.

G. x *monacense* **'Muldoon'** A clone with very striking, strongly dark-blotched leaves.

G. **'Natalie'** (*G. clarkei* 'Kashmir White' x species x *G.* 'Pamir') 45cm (18in) June-August.
An Alan Bremner hybrid, introduced by Catforth Gardens. A low-growing plant with soft lilac-blue flowers freely produced. This is a welcome addition to the few smaller blue flowered geraniums. Front of the border, large rock garden.
Prop: D

G. nepalense E. Afghanistan, Himalayas, China.
A weedy species related to *G. thunbergii;* of no real garden value except perhaps in the wild garden. Dark evergreen leaves usually blotched with purplish brown. Flowers 1cm (½in), white to pale pink on thin trailing stems. Self-sown seedlings can be a nuisance.

G. nervosum (syns *G. strigosum* and *G. viscosissimum* var. *nervosum*). NW America. 30-45cm (12-18in). May onwards.
A variable plant bearing a strong resemblance to *G. viscosissimum* with the

same sticky hairy characteristics, though the basal leaves are smaller. These are light green and broadly fingered with few, smaller stem leaves. Flowers, borne on a single stem, are branched at the top, 2–4cm (1-3in), flat, pale pink to reddish purple with notched petals and dark veins. Some years ago Blooms of Bressingham were offering a small form under the name *G. incisum* (which belongs strictly to *G. oreganum*). Its flowers were a lovely deep rose pink with finely pencilled crimson veins, but numerous self-sown seedlings were generally of poor colour. Border or wild garden in sun or shade. Will grow in dry shade under trees or shrubs.
Prop: D or S

G. 'Nicola' ★ (*G. oxonianum* x *G. psilostemon*) 60cm (2ft). June-September. Alan Bremner hybrid introduced by Catforth Gardens and named after one of Judith Bradshaw's daughters. Although similar to *G.* 'Patricia', 'Nicola' differs in having widely spaced petals revealing the sepals. The star-like flowers are magenta-pink, darkly veined, with a very dark central zone. Border.
Prop: D

G. 'Nimbus' ★ (*G. clarkei* 'Kashmir Purple' x *G. collinum*) 60-90cm (2-3ft). May-July.
A hybrid from Cambridge Botanic Garden, 1978. Introduced by Axletree Nursery. A tall plant with rather lax stems and finely cut feathery foliage, often golden tinted when young. Violet-blue starry flowers 4cm (1½ in) are held well above the leaves. The petals are delicately veined and separated. It looks good when scrambling through taller plants or shrubs in cloud-like profusion. Lovely with *Rosa* x *alba* 'Maiden's Blush'. Back of the border, wild garden.
Prop: D

G. nodosum ★ Central France to Pyrenees, C. Italy, C. of the former Yugoslavia. 30cm (1ft). Spring to autumn.
A modestly charming geranium for woodland or shady border; will colonise under trees in dry soil. Flowers funnel-shaped 2cm (¾-1in), lilac pink with notched petals. Hardly out of flower all summer. There is also a pink flowered form.
Prop: D or S (self-sows in moderation)

G.n. 'Svelte Lilac' has attractively cut leaves and pale-eyed lilac flowers traced with dark red veins and red anthers.

G.n. 'Swish Purple' Dark-veined violet-purple flowers, pale at the centre, are held above deeply cut foliage that is somewhat darker than the type.

G.n. 'Whiteleaf' Raised by the late Lionel Bacon, the name referring to his house, not the leaf colour. The deep purple flowers have each petal finely defined with a white edge.

Geranium nodosum 'Whiteleaf'

G. 'Nora Bremner' (*G. rubifolium* x *G. wallichianum* 'Buxton's Variety') 25cm (10in). June-September. Raised by Alan Bremner and named after his mother. This plant makes leafy mounds of marbled foliage with the same rambling habit as *G.* 'Buxton's Variety'. The beautiful flowers are large, 4cm (1½in), soft violet-blue in colour with a large white centre-piece. The petals are finely veined and separated. Unfortunately it is not easy to propagate as it resents division and cuttings will not root (at least for the writer!) Border or woodland in good, moisture-retentive soil.
Prop: Careful division in spring, if you are sufficiently brave!

G. oreganum W. USA. 60cm (2ft). June-July.
A lovely plant with leaves similar to *G. pratense* making substantial clumps.

Flowers 5cm (1¾ 2in), saucer-shaped and upwardly inclined, deep rose purple and prolific. Border in sun or part shade.
Prop: D or S

G. 'Orkney Pink' (*G. traversii* x *G. sessiliflorum* 'Nigricans' x *oxonianum*) 15cm (6in). June-October.
Raised by Alan Bremner in Orkney. A popular plant forming prostrate mats of bronzy-green leaves, resembling those of *G.* x *oxonianum* in miniature. Quantities of shimmering deep pink flowers 3cm (1¼in) on spreading stems keep going until the frost hits them. Large rock garden, gravel bed in well-drained soil and full sun.
Prop: C

G. orientalitibeticum *G. stapfianum* var. *roseum* misapplied. SW China. 20cm (8in). June-July.
Tuberous rooted. Pretty marbled leaves. Flowers 2.5cm (1in), purplish pink with white centre. Somewhat invasive and best contained in pockets between paving stones.
Prop: T

G. x **oxonianum** * (*G. endressii* x *G. versicolor*)

G. x **o. 'A.T. Johnson'** AGM Slightly shorter than *G. endressii* at 30cm (1ft). Flowers delicate silvery pink, very freely produced.

G. x **o 'Breckland Sunset'** Raised by Jenny and Tim Fuller, The Plantsman's Preference, Norfolk. A strong grower with funnel-shaped flowers of deep glowing carmine-pink, heavily veined with dark red. It flowers over a long period.

G. x **o. 'Claridge Druce'** 45-60cm (18-24in). Extremely vigorous; handsome greyish-green foliage. Flowers large, trumpet-shaped, deep rose pink, strongly veined. An ideal weed-smothering groundcover but should only be introduced to the small garden with caution. Grows practically anywhere!
Prop: D or S (seedlings may vary, but self-sows with abandon)

G. x **o. 'Coronet'** Raised by HPS member, the late Barbara Keuning, in Belgium and introduced by Axletree Nursery. A small form that has very unusual flowers 2cm (¾in) of reddish pink. The stamens are petaloids (like petals in appearance), forming a crown-like structure at the centre of the flower. They have a quaint appeal.

G. x **o. 'Frank Lawley'** Found in Frank's garden at Herterton, Northumberland, by Robin Moss, who named it. A low-growing form 30cm (1ft) with large, pearly salmon-pink flowers.

G. x o. 'Fran's Star' (*G. x o.* 'Southcome Double' x *G. x o.* 'Walter's Gift') 50cm (20in).
Raised by Bleddyn Wynn-Jones (Crûg Farm Plants) and named in memory of Frances, the late wife of HPS member Brian Varley. This geranium has inherited the strongly brown-blotched foliage of *G.* 'Walter's Gift' and flowers similar to *G.* 'Southcombe Double'; rosy pink, semi-double. It prefers a fairly moist soil and if cut down after the first flowering will produce a second flush.
Prop: D

G. x o. 'Hexham Pink' Raised by Robin Moss in Hexham. 45cm (18in). This compact plant has deep lavender-pink bowl-shaped flowers with overlapping lustrous petals without any veining. It is very floriferous over a long period.

G. x o. 'Pat Smallacombe' Raised by Pat in Devon. It has large purplish-pink flowers with a white eye and is very heavily veined.

G. x o. 'Phoebe Noble' From Phoebe's garden on Vancouver Island and distributed by Elke and Ken Knechtel of Rainforest Gardens in B.C. One of the darkest of all *G. x oxonianum* cultivars, having intense magenta-pink, heavily veined flowers – a very fine form.

G. x o. 'Rebecca Moss' Raised by Robin Moss in Northumberland and named after his daughter. A distinct form with very delicate silvery-pink flowers with no veins, deepening with age. Very attractive.

G. x o. 'Rose Clair' 45-60cm (18-24in). Described by Walter Ingwersen as "a clear rose-salmon with just a trace of veining and similar habit to *G.* 'A.T. Johnson'." Unfortunately plants with white veiny flowers are often sold under this name.

G. x o. 'Southcombe Double' 40cm (15in). Originated at Southcombe Garden Plant Nursery in Devon. Flowers 2cm (¾in), semi-double, warm pink similar to *G.* 'Wargrave Pink' - a pretty plant. Not so vigorous as other oxonianum hybrids.
Prop: D (sterile)

G. x o. 'Southcombe Star' Previously thought to be the same as *G. x o.* 'Southcombe Double' but has a more sprawling habit and mauve-pink starry flowers.
Prop: D (sterile)

G. x o. f. *thurstonianum* 45-60cm (18-24in). Flowers with very narrow curiously twisted petals, reddish purple, white at the base and deeply notched. Foliage sometimes blotched, but plants are variable. Interesting rather than beautiful.

G. x o. 'Trevor's White' (Originally known as *G. endressii album*).Raised by Trevor Bath in Woking and named by him. A pure white form with blue-grey anthers. The flowers age to blush pink.

G. x o. 'Walter's Gift' Named after the former garden of Mary Ramsdale, in Essex, where the seedling occurred. A distinctive plant that has heavily blotched chocolate-brown zones spreading from the centre of the leaves. The flowers are pale pink with a network of purplish-crimson veins. An excellent foliage plant that, like all forms of *G. x oxonianum*, benefits from being cut right down after the first flush of flowers.

G. x o. 'Wargrave Pink' AGM A taller cultivar having warm salmon-pink flowers. Vigorous.

G. x o. 'Winscombe' 45cm (18in). Discovered by the late Margery Fish in a Somerset garden; similar in habit to *G. endressii*. Flowers open very pale silvery pink, darkening with age to deep pink, creating a delightful two-tone effect.

G. palmatum AGM (syn. *G. anemonifolium* misapplied) Madeira. 35-90cm (14-36in). Summer.
Resembles *G. canariense,* but with hardly any rosette stem and greener stalks. Rosettes very large, leaves can be 30cm (1ft) or more across. Flowers 1-1 ½in (approx. 3 cm), very prolific, mauvish pink, crimson centre. May need winter protection in all colder areas. Makes a showy pot-plant.
Prop: S

G. palustre * E. and C. Europe. 30–45cm (12-18in). All summer.
A low growing, bushy plant. Basal leaves light green, remaining fresh looking even in drought conditions. Flowers 3cm (1-1½in), trumpet-shaped bright magenta pink, with dark veins, white at the centre and violet anthers. Useful in the border for its long flowering period, trailing over plants that are out of flower.
Prop: S (self-sows freely)

G. 'Patricia' * (*G. endressii* x *G. psilostemon*) 90cm (3ft). One of Alan Bremner's hybrids and named after Mrs Patricia Doughty. Resembles *G. psilostemon* though the 4cm (1½in) flowers are a little softer in colour and are carried over a canopy of very large leaves 23cm (9in) in width. It makes an eye-catching plant for the border in full sun.
Prop: D

G. peloponnesiacum Greece. 45-60cm (18-24in). May-June.
Pretty, velvety wrinkled leaves dying down after flowering, re-appearing in

autumn. Flowers 4cm (1½in) clusters on long stems, upward facing, slatey blue. Petals deeply notched and veiny. A dainty plant for rock garden or border.
Prop: S

G. phaeum * Mountains of S. & C. Europe. 60cm (2ft). May-July.
The 'Mourning Widow' geranium, so called because of its unusually dark, nodding flowers. Leaves divided and sometimes blotched with purplish brown in the notches. Flowers 2.5cm (1in), flattish, very sombre dark maroon, white at centre. Petals often slightly frilled round the edge. Excellent for quite dry shady areas, where it will colonise and hybridise where other forms are grown.

G.p. '**Album**' A delightful pure white.

G.p. '**Blue Shadow**' Raised and introduced by Jenny and Tim Fuller, The Plantsman's Preference Nursery. The flower colour of this geranium is difficult to define, described by Jenny as "amethyst with a blue appearance", but changes in different coloured lights. Said to be the bluest form of *G. phaeum*.

G.p. '**Calligrapher**' Raised by John Sirkett in Cornwall. This distinctive form has frilled and pointed petals, each edged with a band of bluish-purple and having the same colour at the base, with pale area in between, and highlighted by deep violet veins. The leaves are strongly marked with dark brownish purple in the notches.

G.p. '**Joan Baker**' collected by A.W.A. (Bill) Baker and named after his wife. A tall plant with large 2.5cm (1in) flowers of pale lavender blue, darker at the centre.

G.p. '**Lily Lovell**' A beautiful large flowered form of rich purple mauve, raised by Trevor Bath in Woking, Surrey and named after his mother. The foliage is somewhat lighter in colour than other cultivars.

G.p. var. ***lividum*** Very pale mauve.

G.p. '**Margaret Wilson**' This has variegated foliage that appears in spring in shades of white and yellow, remaining stable and impressive through the season. Flowers are bluish-purple.

G.p. '**Rose Madder**' Raised by Trevor Bath. The name was suggested by Mary Caröe of Vann in Surrey, referring to the colour, which is a deep brownish-pink and unique in geraniums. The leaves are spotted red in the divisions with smaller spots round the edge.

G.p. '**Samobor**' Collected in Croatia by Elizabeth Strangman. A superb foliage plant named after the village where it was found. Each rich green leaf is heavily zoned with dark chocolate blotches. The flowers are a typical dark purple but on shorter stems. Best grown in shade, preferably in moist soil.

G.p. 'Stillingfleet Ghost' Raised and introduced by Vanessa Cook of Stillingfleet Nursery in Yorkshire. The large, lavender-grey flowers have a spectral appearance, especially on a misty day.

G.p. 'Variegatum' Leaves splashed irregularly with cream and touches of bright, reddish pink.
Prop: D or S (variable)

G. 'Philippe Vapelle' * (*G. renardii* x *G. platypetalum*) 38cm (15in). June-July.
The same cross was made by Ivan Louvette in Belgium and Alan Bremner in Orkney, resulting in identical plants. Beautiful soft, hairy deciduous leaves with velvet texture, similar to but larger than those of *G. renardii*, form substantial mounds. Complementing the foliage, the flowers are bluish-purple, strongly veined and wide-open, with notched petals. Front of the border in sun.
Prop: D

G. platyanthum (syn. *G. eriostemon*) NE Asia, E. Tibet, W. China, Korea and Japan. 45-60cm (18-24in). May-June.
A handsome, hairy geranium with large, wrinkled shallowly lobed leaves, colouring well in the autumn. Flowers 3cm (1-1½in), nearly flat, in dense clusters on erect stems; slatey-mauvish pink with small white centre. Sometimes disparagingly described as 'muddy coloured' or "ill defined purple" though it can be both interesting and pleasing. Border, woodland, wild garden in sun or part shade.
Prop:D or S

G. platypetalum Caucasus. 30-45cm (12-18in). June-July.
A hairy plant somewhat similar to *G. ibericum*, but leaves not so deeply cut and less sharply toothed. Flowers 4cm (1½in), deep violet blue with strong dark veins. Border and ground cover in sun or part shade.
Prop:D or S

G. pogonanthum SW China, W. & N. Burma. 45-60cm(18-24in). July-September.
Very attractive both in leaf and flower. Forms clumps of lightish-green, marbled leaves. Flowers 3cm (1-1½in), dusky pink with narrow, reflexed petals like small cyclamen. Beautiful and unusual. Takes a year or two to establish and then needs regular replanting if the roots work their way to the surface. Border, wild garden. Sun or shade.
Prop: D or S

G. polyanthes Himalayas, SW China. 38-45cm (15-18in). July.
Grows from knobbly brown tuber-like roots, which tend to push their way out of the soil and need recovering Leaves small, rounded, divided and fleshy. Flowers 2.5cm (1in) funnel-shaped, very bright shiny pink. A pretty plant for large rock garden, but difficult to keep in cultivation, often dying out after two or three years.
Prop: S (easy)

G. pratense * N. Europe, Asia. 60-90cm (2-3ft). June-July.
Our well-loved meadow cranesbill, a wonderful sight when colonising vast areas of roadside. It will do the same in the garden, making large clumps of handsomely divided leaves and quantities of saucer-shaped flowers 4cm(1½in) in lovely shades from deep violet blue, pink, pale blue and white with varying degrees of veining, borne on tall branching stems. Border (may need support), meadow, light woodland. There are a number of desirable garden forms.
Prop: D (seed will be variable, though all but the doubles are prolific seeders)

G.p. f. ***albiflorum*** The name for the white flowered forms, both wild and cultivated.

G.p. f. ***a.*** **'Galactic'** Rather shorter, darker leaf and pure, milky white flowers.

G.p. f. ***a.*** **'Plenum Album'** Rather small, loosely petalled rosettes of 'off white' flowers tinged with violet. Not easy to grow, needing rich soil and regular dividing.
Prop: D (sterile)

G.p. **'Bittersweet'** From Monksilver Nursery in Cambridgeshire. The delicate cup-shaped flowers are very pale lavender-pink with translucent veins and black anthers. When young the leaves are tinged with purple, changing to green when mature.

G.p. **'Mrs Kendall Clark'** AGM An exquisite shade of pearly blue grey, flushed with soft pink.

G.p. **'Plenum Caeruleum'** Copious loosely petalled rosettes of lavender-blue flowers tinged with pink, over a long period from June to August. Prone to mildew in dry soil. Benefits from regular division. Lovely with grey or silver leaved plants - a 'must' for the border!
Prop: D (sterile)

G.p. **'Plenum Violaceum'** AGM (probably syn. *G.p.* 'Purpureum Plenum')
Perfectly formed tight pompons of rich violet, a bit later than *G.p.* 'Plenum Caeruleum', not quite so vigorous.
Prop: D (sterile)

Geranium pratense 'Plenum Violaceum'

G.p. Victor Reiter Strain Seed from this strain, developed by the late Victor Reiter in America, will result in variable seedlings from plain green, through bronzy-green, to very dark purple (the latter being the most sought after). This strain has been named **Midnight Reiter**, producing plants that tend to be slow growing and shorter than the typical *G. pratense*, needing moist fertile soil. They also bloom earlier. The dark leaves, combined with lavender-blue flowers (though these may vary in colour) look stunning associated with silver or glaucous foliage plants. The dark forms have been given the trade name of **Purple Haze** by Plant World Seed of Newton Abbot in Devon.

G.p. **'Silver Queen'** A tall, strong-growing plant of palest silvery blue, but the description from the Wisley Trials Report, "white with a tinge of very pale violet" seems to be nearer the plant generally sold under this name. Some forms are enhanced by prominent black anthers.

G.p. subsp. ***stewartianum*** **'Elizabeth Yeo'** Collected by Dr S.K. Rainer in Kashmir and named by Dr Peter Yeo after his wife. A tall plant, 90cm (3ft), flowering earlier than other forms of *G. pratense* in May-June and spasmodically through to September. Charming large pink flowers are poised gracefully above the well-cut foliage.

G.p. **'Striatum'** (syn. *G. p.* 'Bicolor') Interesting and attractive variant. Flowers basically white, erratically streaked with violet.
Prop: S (comes true)

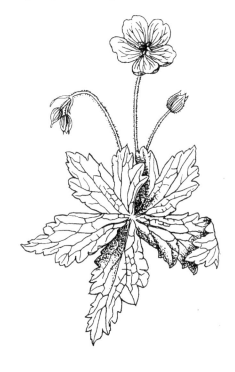

Geranium pulchrum

G. procurrens * Himalayas. July onwards.
Low growing, rampant ground cover for dry areas. Sending out very long prostrate stems, which root at the leaf joints. Leaves wrinkled and faintly marbled. Flowers 2.5cm (1in) subdued purple, black at centre. Will weave

through shrubs or cover large areas under specimen trees. This geranium should carry a warning 'Beware of Take Over'!
Prop: rooted pieces easily transplanted.

G. psilostemon AGM * (syn. *G. armenum*) NE Turkey, SW Caucasus. 90-120cm (3-4ft). June-August.
A stunning border plant with elegant, very large, deeply cut leaves, turning brilliant red in autumn. Flowers 4cm (1½in), bowl-shaped, intense magenta crimson accentuated by a black central zone and dark veins. Best in sun but will tolerate some shade. Can be toned down by planting in association with pastel shades and silver foliage. *G.p.* 'Bressingham Flair' is a paler form, light magenta and a little shorter.
Prop: D or S

G. pulchrum South Africa. 90cm (3ft). July-August.
A lovely foliage sub-shrub. Stems woody and quite thick at the base. Leaves soft, velvety, silvery grey green, undersides covered with silvery silky hairs - almost white; handsomely fingered and sharply serrated. Flowers 3cm (1-1½in), mauvish-pink, sometimes white at centre. Has survived four winters outside in Somerset and -6°C or more of frost! Sun or light shade. Border or bank.
Prop: C or S

G. pylzowianum W. China. 15-25cm (6-10in). May-June.
Travels rapidly by chains of small tubers. Leaves rounded, finely dissected. Flowers 2cm (1in), deep clear pink. Can be a pest in the rock garden, and best kept away from precious plants: in containers, paving or edge of path in sun.
Prop: T

G. pyrenaicum SW & W. Europe. 30cm(1ft). May onwards.
Mounds of nicely rounded, evergreen leaves. Flowers 2cm (¾in), mauvish pink with notched petals freely produced on thin stems. Rather too weedy for anything but the wild garden. *G. p.* f. *albiflorum* is a pretty, starry white flowered form.
Prop: S (self sows abundantly)

G.p. 'Bill Wallis' Raised and introduced by the late Bill Wallis of the Useful Plant Company in Cambridgeshire. A very popular form, smaller and more compact than the type: 30cm (1ft). Masses of small, strikingly attractive rich purple flowers. At plant sales it sells like the proverbial hot cakes when in flower.

G.p. 'Isparta' A recent introduction collected in the Isparta Province of Turkey by Dr Peter Yeo. This is a taller plant: 60cm (2ft) that has pretty pale blue white-eyed flowers from early summer into autumn.

G. reflexum Italy, the former Yugoslavia, N. Greece. 45-60cm (18-24in).
May-June.
Similar to *G. phaeum* with fresh green leaves, usually blotched dark
purplish brown where divisions meet. Flowers 2cm (¾in), nodding rosy
mauve, strongly reflexed, narrow petals, white at base. Ground cover or
shady corner.
Prop: D or S

G. refractum Himalayas, N. Burma, SW China. 45-60cm (18-24in).
Not in cultivation until recently, but seed from Nepal now being
distributed. Deeply divided, sometimes marbled leaves. Flowers nodding,
white or pink, narrow reflexed petals, red stamens. Distinguished by purple
glandular hairs on the upper parts.

G. renardii AGM Caucasus. 30cm (1ft). June.
A lovely foliage plant. Leaves a soft sage green, velvety to the touch, with a
distinctive scalloped shape. Flowers large, white, etched with purple veins.
Petals widely spaced. Often a shy flowerer, said to do better in poor soil in
sun or part shade. Rock garden, low wall, paving, front of the border.
Prop: D or S

***G.r.* 'Whiteknights'** This is actually a blue-flowered form raised by
Reading University on their Whiteknights Botanic Garden estate from seed
collected in the wild. More robust than the type and not so compact. The 4
cm (1½ in) violet-blue flowers are heavily veined with purplish violet and
tend to flop rather untidily over the typical sage-green foliage.

G. richardsonii Western N. America. 30-60cm (1-2ft).
May onwards.
Pleasing clumps of deeply divided, shiny green leaves with pointed lobes.
Flowers 3cm (1-1½in), flat white or tinged with pink, lightly veined. Likes
plenty of moisture in wild garden or pond-side in sun.
Prop: D or S

G. x riversleaianum (*G. endressii* x *G. traversii*)

***G. x r.* 'Mavis Simpson'** Makes wide mats of 22cm (9in) high grey-green
leaves covered with endless, silvery shell-pink flowers on thin trailing stems
all summer into autumn. Seems to be hardier than *G. x r.* 'Russell
Prichard'. Front of the border, rock garden, low wall or bank in sun.
Lovely with purple foliage plants.
Prop: D (sterile)

***G. x r.* 'Russell Prichard'** AGM 20cm (8in) mounds of small silvery
grey-green foliage. Flowers 3cm (1¼in), bright magenta pink on trailing
stems, prolifically produced from July onwards. Not reliably hardy. Try

planting at a slight downward angle beneath overhanging rock to protect crowns from winter wet. Similar situations to *G.* 'Mavis Simpson'.
Prop: D (sterile)

G. robustum South Africa. 60cm (2ft). All summer.
A reasonably hardy sub-shrub, stems woody at the base. Lovely ferny grey-green leaves silvery on the underside. Flowers 3cm (1-1½in), mauvish pink or pale purple, shallowly notched petals. Withstands drought well and has survived outside for the past six years in Somerset, before that several years in Surrey. Border in sun. Effective with red-leaved berberis, *Heuchera* 'Palace Purple' and *Crocus speciosus*.
Prop: C or S (self sows occasionally)

***G.* 'Rosie Crûg'** (*G.* Crûg Strain x *G. lambertii*) A recent introduction from Crûg Farm Nursery. Appealing, open, slightly nodding, flowers are very pale and finely veined with rose-pink from a stronger pink central zone; low mats of pewter-bronze foliage. Rock garden, gravel in full sun. Needs sharp drainage.
Prop: C

***G.* Rozanne** = **'Gerwat'** (*G. wallichaianum* 'Buxton's Variety' x *G. himalyense*)
A seedling found in the garden of Donald and Rozanne Waterer and introduced by Blooms of Bressingham. The plant proved very difficult to propagate, taking several years of trialing before being launched as the star geranium of Chelsea 2000. It is very vigorous with wide-spreading stems up to 120cm (4ft), having foliage of the *G. wallichianum* type, which colours well with age. The 4cm (1¾in) flowers, are of a gorgeous deep violet-blue merging to a pale pinkish central zone and are enhanced by prominent black anthers. The petals have a silky sheen with overtones of purplish red. Front of the border, tub, or even a hanging basket in full sun.
Prop: Cuttings could be tried.

G. rubescens (biennial) Madeira. 60-90cm (2-3ft). May onwards.
Resembles a large herb robert. Flower and leaf stalks beetroot red from impressive rosette. Flowers 2.5cm (1in) numerous, bright pink with dark centre. Reasonably hardy in a sheltered corner in light soil, sun or shade, naturalising where happy. Sometimes affected by virus that distorts the petals (in which case the plants should be destroyed).

***G.* 'Russell Prichard'** see *G.* x *riversleaianum*

***G.* 'Salome'** (*G. lambertii* x *G. procurrens*) 90cm (3ft) July-September.
Raised from a seedling by Elizabeth Strangman of Washfield Nursery in Kent. Long trailing, non-rooting, stems emerge from a comparatively small

mound of gold-tinged, marbled leaves. The large flowers, 3cm (1¼ in), are pale violet-purple with deeper veins blending into a striking near-black central eye. Border or woodland. Shade in good soil but happy in sun if the roots are shaded.

Prop: Difficult; cuttings a possibility.

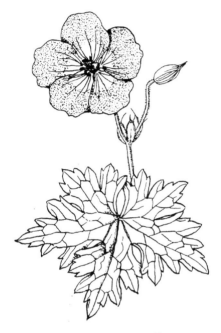

Geranium Rozanne (*G.* 'Gerwat')

G. sanguineum ★ Europe, Caucasus, N. Turkey. 22-30cm (9-12in). May onwards.

The 'Bloody Cranesbill', though not blood-red! Forms wide mats of tangled, leafy stems. Leaves small, rounded, finely cut, turning brilliant shades in autumn. Flowers 3cm (1-1½in), saucer-shaped, purple magenta all summer. Front of the border, rock garden, low walls, paving.

Prop: D or S (seedlings variable)

G.s. 'Album' AGM A good pure white, taller than the type, rather spindly stems and less compact.

G.s. 'Ankum's Pride' Raised by Coen Jansen in Holland from a seedling of *G.s.* 'Jubilee Pink' and named after his village. A neat form that has bright pink flowers, darkly veined.

G.s. 'Belle of Herterton' Found by Robin Moss in Frank Lawley's garden at Herterton House, Northumberland and introduced by Crûg Farm Nursery. A very pretty, compact plant with luminous rose-pink cup-shaped flowers and overlapping heavily veined petals fading to white.

G.s. 'Glenluce' Discovered by A. T. Johnson in Scotland. Beautiful, large rose pink flowers.

G.s. 'Holden' (syn. *G.s.* 'Holden's Variety') Close mats of small leaves and bright pure pink flowers.

G.s. 'Jubilee Pink' Raised by Jack Drake in Scotland. Compact growth, bright magenta pink flowers.

G.s. 'Max Frei' A seedling found in the garden of Max Frei in Switzerland, making compact mounds of dark green foliage covered with large bright pinkish-purple flowers.The leaves colour well in autumn.

G.s. var. ***striatum*** AGM (syn. *G. lancastriense*) One of the best from Walney Island in Lancashire (now Cumbria). Large, very pale pink flowers (almost white) with pink veins, non-stop all summer until the frosts.

G. sessiliflorum subsp. ***novae-zelandiae*** New Zealand. 7cm (3in). June onwards.
Neat rosettes of small rounded green leaves and tiny 1cm (½in) white flowers. Rock garden, scree, trough or gravel path.
Prop: S

G. s. subsp. ***n.-z.*'Nigricans'** * A fascinating dark-leaved form, varying from pale bronze to very dark brown. Self-sows moderately. Seems to like the peat bed.

G. shikokianum S. Japan, Korea. 20-40cm (8-16in). July onwards.
Compact clumps of deeply cut, light green leaves, often with yellowish-green marbling, pale and glossy on the under sides. Good autumn colour.. Flowers on longish stems, funnel-shaped, 2.5cm (1in) pink with white central area, netted with purple veins. Dislikes hot dry conditions, best in shade, scrambling through low shrubs.
Prop: D or S

G. sibiricum E. & C. Europe, CIS, China, Japan, W. Himalayas.
A weedy sprawling plant with light green leaves and small 1cm (½in) white or pale pink flowers. No real garden value.

G. sinense SW China. 60cm (2ft). July-August.
A fascinating and unusual plant of great distinction. Leaves deeply divided, shiny olive green and faintly marbled, on reddish stems. Flowers 2cm (¾in) similar in shape to *G. phaeum* very dark (almost black) velvety

reflexed petals, coral at the base, black anthers and crimson-red stigma; deserves close inspection. Plants rather slow to establish, building up to a substantial mound. Shade and moist soil. Curiously attractive to wasps.
Prop: D or S

G. 'Sirak' ★ (*G. gracile* x *G. ibericum*) 45cm (18in). June-July.
Plants of this cross raised independently by Alan Bremner in Orkney and Hans Simon in Germany are identical. A splendidly free-flowering plant having large flowers like those of *G.* x *magnificum* but mallow-pink in colour with the eye-lash veins of *G. gracile*, over sturdy clumps of leaves resembling those of *G. ibericum*. A second crop of flowers may appear in late summer. Border, light woodland in shade.
Prop: D

G. soboliferum CIS, Manchuria, mountains of C. & S. Japan. 30-40cm (12-15in). July-Sept.
Small clumps of finely cut feathery leaves. Flowers 4cm (1½in), saucer-shaped, reddish purple with dark veins, notched petals. Needs plenty of moisture in full sun.
Prop: D or S

G. 'Spinners' ★ (*G. pratense* x ?) 90cm (3ft). June-July. Raised by Peter Chappell at Spinners Nursery in Hampshire from seed collected by the late Marvin Black in USA. The exact parentage of this magnificent plant is unknown. Originally distributed under various incorrect names (i.e. *G. bergianum*, *G. pratense* 'Kashmir Purple', and *G. clarkei* 'Kashmir Purple') it was eventually given the cultivar name of 'Spinners'. The wonderful 3cm (1¼in) bowl-shaped flowers of an intense rich purple-blue are upturned over a mass of finely cut foliage. Border, weaving through neighbouring plants in sun.
Prop: D

G. stapfianum SW China, SE Tibet. 15cm (6in). June.
A dwarf plant, spreading by underground stolons. Leaves small, kidney-shaped, deeply cut and marbled. Leaf and flower stalks red. Flowers 4cm (1½in), saucer-shaped, deep magenta with dark red veins and notched petals. Not an easy plant in cultivation. Rock garden, scree, alpine house. (This is not the geranium sold as *G. stapfianum roseum* for which see *G. orientalitibeticum*.)
Prop: D or S

G. 'Stephanie' (*G. peloponnesiacum* x *G.renardii*?) 36cm (14in). April-May.
Puzzled when my plant, acquired as *G. peloponnesiacum*, failed to die down after flowering, I gave a piece to Judith Bradshaw and we managed to track

it down to Edinburgh Botanic Garden, where it had been grown as *G. peloponnesiacum* but was in fact a chance seedling, probably with *G. renardii* as a parent (certainly it has similar leaves). Beautiful large pale lilac-blue flowers are effectively traced with dark veins. Judith was given permission by the Edinburgh Botanic Garden to name the plant after one of her granddaughters. Front of border, large rock garden in full sun.
Prop: D

***G.* 'Sue Crûg'** (*G. oxonianum* x *G.* 'Salome') 38cm (15in). June- September. Raised by Bleddyn Wynn-Jones at Crûg Farm Plants and named after his wife. Has flowers similar to 'Salome' though larger, at 4cm (1½in), and with purplish-pink separated petals, strongly veined with near-white streaks down the centres. The dark central eye is less prominent. Mid-green, slightly marbled, foliage resembles that of the other parent, *G.* x *oxonianum*, and is on trailing stems from a basal mound. Front of border in reasonable soil that is not too hot and dry.
Prop: Not tried, but careful division in spring should be possible.

Geranium 'Sue Crûg'

G. Summer Skies = **G. 'Gernic'** (*G. pratense* x *G. himalayense* 'Plenum')
60cm (2ft). June-July.
Raised by Kevin Nicholson in Wisbech and introduced by Bressingham
Nursery. Although the first flowering of the writer's plant did not live up to
expectations it is, after three years, delightful. Shorter than the other double
forms of *G. pratense* and coming into bloom earlier. Fully double flowers
are a pretty lavender blue with overtones of pink fading rather dismally to
ecru. Border in full sun and fertile soil.
Prop: D

G. swatense Swat division of Pakistan. 30cm (1ft). All summer.
A low growing, sprawling plant from a thick taproot, mottled leaves on
long thin reddish stems. Flowers 4cm (1½in) rather flat, purplish pink with
purple anthers, but variable. Not easy to please and liable to die out. Rock
garden or wall in sun or part shade.
Prop: D or S

G. sylvaticum * Europe, N. Turkey. 60-75cm (24-30in). May-June and
often later.
The wood cranesbill. An upright geranium developing fine clumps of
broadly fingered, lightish green leaves, attractively lobed and toothed.
Flowers 2.5cm (1in) saucer-shaped, purplish violet with white centres, in
profusion.

G.s. 'Album' AGM 45cm (18in), a beautiful pure white form with large
pale green leaves. A valuable addition to the White Garden.

G.s. 'Baker's Pink' A natural pink variant collected in the Swiss Alps
near Wengen by A. W. A. 'Bill' Baker. An especially good tall form with
large, clear shell-pink blooms and a long flowering period,

G.s. 'Mayflower' An improved clone with larger, pale violet blue, white-
centred flowers. Lovely with spring flowers and bulbs.

G. sylvaticum subsp. **sylvaticum** var. **wanneri** has flowers of
plummy pink with rose red veins.
Prop: D or S (seedlings will be variable though *G.s.. 'Album'* seems to
come true)

G. thunbergii N. China, Taiwan, Japan. 22cm (9in). July-October.
A vigorous, sprawling plant. Leaves lightish green with dark blotches,
where divisions meet. Semi-evergreen. Flowers 1.5cm (½-¾in) varying
from white to purplish pink over a long period. Rather weedy but useful
ground cover for dry shade.
Prop: D or S

G. traversii var. *elegans* Chatham Islands. 15-20cm (6-8in). June-September.

Compact rosettes of silver green, beautifully fashioned cut leaves. Flowers 2.5cm (1in), saucer-shaped, lovely milky pink and finely veined on leafy stems which tend to flop and lie on the surface of the soil. Rock garden, scree, alpine house in well-drained gritty soil in full sun. Not completely hardy, needing some protection in winter.

Prop: S (self-sown seedlings occasionally appear)

G. tuberosum Mediterranean. 20-25cm (8-10in). May.

Grows from moderately spreading tubers, sending up finely cut ferny leaves in spring, dying down in summer. Flowers 2.5cm (1in), purplish pink with darker veins on erect stems. Rock garden or scree in sun.

Prop: D or S

G. versicolor ★ (syn. *G. striatum*) Europe. 45cm (18in). May.

A bushy plant similar to *G. endressii* forming hummocks of light green, blotched leaves that remain fresh in winter. Dainty flowers, trumpet-shaped 2.5cm (1in), white with a network of fine magenta veins. Good ground cover for sun or shade. Hybridizes freely with *G. endressii.*

Prop: D (seedlings will be variable)

G. viscosissimum Western N. America. 30-60cm (1-2ft). June and often later.

An attractive, sticky plant with large hairy divided leaves and sharply toothed segments, similar to *G. nervosum*. Flowers 3cm (1¼-1½in), bright rose pink to purple in clusters on strong branching stems. Border in sun.

Prop: D or S

G. wallichianum **'Buxton's Variety'** AGM (syn. *G.w.* 'Buxton's Blue') Himalayas. 30cm (1ft). July onwards.

Originated in the garden of E. C. Buxton in N. Wales. A great favourite, having long, leafy trailing stems. Leaves shallowly divided and marbled. Flowers 3cm (1-1½in) saucer-shaped, beautiful sky blue with large, clean white centre. Although said to require a cool root run, it has thrived and flowered prolifically in hot, dry summers. Rock garden, under shrubs, trailing over low walls.

Prop: S (comes true, but advisable to select seedlings with best blue flowers)

G.w. **'Syabru'** Collected in Nepal by Edward Needham and named after the Sherpa village where it was found; introduced by Washfield Nursery. A strong grower developing mounds of dark green leaves topped by brilliant pure magenta darkly veined flowers on trailing stems. It has a longer flowering period than *G.w.* 'Buxton's Variety'. In the wild, *G. wallichianum* is very variable and several colour variants are becoming available. The most outstanding of these is *G.w.* 'Chadwell's Pink'. With lovely soft pink flowers – if you can find the true plant!

G. wlassovianum * E. Siberia, Mongolia, Far East, CIS, N. China. 30-45cm (12-18in). July-August.

A clump former with attractive foliage emerging pinkish bronze in spring. Mature leaves dusky green tinged with brown, velvety in texture, assuming brilliant red autumn colour, darkening to purplish brown before dying away. Flowers 3cm (1¼-1in), deep purple violet with darker feathered veins and small white central area. Border, wild garden, ground cover where not excessively dry.

Prop: D or S

G. yesoense C. & N. Japan, Kuril Islands. 30-45cm (12-18in). June-August.

A bushy plant similar to *G. dahuricum*. Leaves very deeply and sharply cut. Flowers 3cm (1¼in), saucer-shaped, pink with darker veins, or white. Not a particularly garden worthy plant, but suitable for light woodland or wild garden in moisture retentive soil.

Prop: D or S

G. yunnanense SW China, N. Burma. 45-60cm (18-24in). June-July.

Compact rootstock, leaves deeply divided, yellowish green and marbled. Flowers 3cm (1-1½in), nodding, bowl-shaped, a lovely deep pink with dark anthers, not easy to grow in south of England. Flowering stems lax. Woodland or wild garden. Sun or part shade.

Prop: D or S

ANNUALS

Of the annual geraniums, several are really only of interest to the collector, having very small flowers and weedy habits. Limitations of space within this booklet have confined descriptions to one or two personal favourites. However, I must mention the herb Robert, *G. robertianum* so pretty and delightful in both pink and white forms. I would not like to be without it, but there are times when I curse its proliferation! *G.r.* 'Celtic White' is smaller, forming rosettes of pale green, parsley-like leaves. It has small, pure white flowers, but is equally generous with its seedlings.

REFERENCES

Ingwersen, W. *The Genus Geranium* 1946.

Yeo, Peter F. *Hardy Geraniums* 1985, 1992.

Clifton, R.T.F. *Geranium Family Species Check List Part 2* 1992 The Geraniaceae Group

Victor, David X. (Registrar,) *Geranium Register of Cultivar Names* May, 2000 The Geraniaceae Group

van der Werff, Dirk. *New, Rare & Unusual Plants* Aquilegia Publishing (magazine)

Geranium pratense 'Plenum Caeruleum'

Further Reading

Bath, Trevor & Jones, Joy. *The Gardener's Guide to Growing Hardy Geraniums.* David & Charles, 1994.

Chivers, Susan & Woloszynska, Suzanne. *The Cottage Garden: Margery Fish at East Lambrook Manor.* John Murray, 1990.

Evrard, Dominic, *L' Essentiel sur les Geraniums Vivaces* (SNHF, 84 Rue de Grenelle, 75007, Paris) 1997. (in French).

Fish, Margery. *Gardening in the Shade.* Faber, 1983.

Fish, Margery. *Ground Cover Plants.* Faber, 1980.

Hibberd, David. *Hardy Geraniums.* Wisley Handbook, RHS, 1994.

Thomas, Graham Stuart. *Perennial Garden Plants.* Dent, 1976.

Yeo, Peter F. *Hardy Geraniums.* Batsford, 1992

Specialist Societies

The Geranium Group of the Hardy Plant Society (open to members of the HPS only)
Administrator: Mrs Pam Adams,
Little Orchard, Great Comberton, Nr. Pershore, Worcs. WR10 3DP
The British Pelargonium and Geranium Society
Honorary Secretaries: Mr and Mrs R. Helyar,
134 Montrose Avenue, Welling, Kent DA16 2QY
The Geraniaceae Group
Secretary: Ms Penny Clifton,
9 Waingate Bridge Cottages, Haverigg, Cumbria LA18 4NF

National Collections of Hardy Geraniums

Mrs J. Bradshaw
Cherry Tree Lodge Nursery, Catforth Gardens, Roots Lane, Catforth, Preston, Lancashire PR4 OJB
D. Browne
Coombland Gardens, Coneyhurst, Billingshurst, Sussex RH14 9DG
Andrew Norton
New House Barn, Barrington, Ilminster, Somerset, TA19 OJD
University Botanic Garden, Cambridge
Cory Lodge, Bateman Street, Cambridge, CB2 1JF

Websites: *(Andrew Norton)*: www.hardygeraniums.com
(The Hardy Plant Society): www.hardy-plant.org.uk
For Websites of individual nurseries see *The RHS Plant Finder*

Where to buy Geraniums

UNITED KINGDOM ($n.m.o.$) = No mail order

The Beth Chatto Gardens Ltd
Elmstead Market, Colchester, Essex CO7 7BD

Beeches Nursery (Kevin Marsh)
Village Centre, Ashdon, Saffron Walden, Essex CB10 2HB

Birkshead Cottage Garden Nursery (Mrs Christine Liddle)
Birkshead Lane, nr. Sunniside, Newcastle-upon-Tyne, NE16 5EL ($n.m.o.$)

Blackthorn Nursery (A.R. and S. B. White)
Kilmeston, Alresford, Hampshire S024 0NL ($n.m.o.$)

Blooms of Bressingham
Diss, Norfolk IP 22 2AB

Cally Gardens (M.C. Wickenden)
Gatehouse of Fleet, Castle Douglas, Dumfries and Galloway DG7 2DJ

Charter House Nursery (John Ross)
2 Nunwood, Dumfries, Dumfries and Galloway DG2 0HX

Cherry Tree Lodge Nursery (Judith Bradshaw)
Catforth Gardens, Roots Lane, Catforth, Preston, Lancashire PR4 0JB ($n.m.o.$)

Coombland Gardens (David Browne)
Coombland, Coneyhurst, Billingshurst, West Sussex RH14 9DG

Corsley Mill (B.E.P. Quest-Ritson)
Highfield House, Shrewton, Salisbury, Wiltshire SP3 4BU (*mail order winter only*)

Croftway Nursery (Graham Spencer)
Yapton Road, Barnham, Bognor Regis, West Sussex PO22 0BH

Crûg Farm Plants (B. Wynn-Jones)
Griffiths' Crossing, near Caernarfon, Gwynedd LL55 1TU ($n.m.o.$)

Eastgrove Cottage Garden Nursery (Malcolm and Carol Skinner)
Sankyns Green, near Shrawley, Little Witley, Worcestershire WR6 6LQ ($n.m.o.$)

East Lambrook Manor Gardens Nursery
East Lambrook, South Petherton, Somerset, TA13 5HL

Elworthy Cottage Garden Plants (Mrs J.M. Spiller)
Elworthy Cottage, Elworthy, Lydeard St Lawrence, Taunton, Somerset
TA4 3PX ($n.m.o.$)

Glebe Cottage Plants (Carol Klein)
Pixie Lane, Warkleigh, Umberleigh, Devon EX37 9DH ($n.m.o.$)

Henllys Lodge Plants (Mrs E. Lane)
Henllys Lodge, Beaumaris, Anglesey, Gwynedd, LL58 8HU

Hunts Court Garden and Nursery (T.K. & M.M.Marshall)
North Nibley, Dursely, Gloucestershire GL11 6DZ (*n.m.o.*)

Kaytie Fisher (Kaytie Fisher)
The Nursery, South End Cottage, Long Reach, Ockham, Surrey GU23 6PF
(*may be moving in 2001*)

Mill Cottage Plants (Sally Gregson)
The Mill, Henley Lane, Wookey, near Wells, Somerset BA5 lAP

Monksilver Nursery (Joe Sharman and Alan Leslie)
Oakington Road, Cottenham, Cambridgeshire CB4 4TW

The Nursery Further Afield (Gerald Sinclair)
Evenley Road, Mixbury, near Brackley, Northamptonshire NN13 5YR (*n.m.o.*)

The Plantsman's Preference (Jenny and Tim Fuller)
Lynwood, Hopton Road, Garboldisham, Diss, Norfolk IP22 2QN

Rosie's Garden Plants (J C A Violet)
Rochester Road, Aylesford, Kent ME20 7EB

Rushfields of Ledbury (B. and J. Homewood)
Ross Road, Ledbury, Herefordshire HR8 2LP

Spinners (Peter Chappell)
Boldre, Lymington, Hampshire S041 5QE. (*n.m.o.*)

Stillingfleet Lodge Nurseries (Vanessa Cook)
Stillingfleet, Yorkshire Y04 6HW

Usual and Unusual Plants (Jennie Maillard)
Onslow House, Magham Down, Hailshaw, East Sussex BN27 1PL (*n.m.o.*)

BELGIUM
Guido van de Steen
Kapellekouter, 9230 Maasemen-Wetteren

Jardiniart-van Mulders
Meerstraat 11, 3018 Wijgmaal

Koen van Poucke
Heistraat 106, 9100 St Niklaas

Kwekerij Sollya, Koen Delaey
Proosdijstraat 56, 8020 Hertsberge

Noël Portier
Margaretha van Vlaanderenstraat 27, 8310 St Kruis (Brugge)

Plantenkwekerij De Wilgenbroek, Maurice Vergote
Wilgenbroekstraat 60, 8020 Oostkamp

Vaste-Plantenkwekerij Jan Spruyt-van der Jeugd
Mustenveld 50, 9255 Bruggenhout

THE NETHERLANDS
Kwekerij De Hessenhof
Hessenweg 41, 6718 TC Ede

Kwekerij Coen Jansen
Ankummer Es 15, 7722 RD Dalfsen
Kwekerij Oudolf
Broekstraat 17, 6999 DE Hummelo
Kwekerij Ploeger
Blauwkapelseweg 73, 3731 EB De Bilt

NORTH AMERICA
Canyon Creek Nursery (John Whittlesey)
3527 Dry Creek Road, Oroville, CA 95965

Cricklewood Nursery (Dan and Evie Douglas)
11907 Nevens Road, Snohomish, WA 98290

Fancy Fronds (Judith Jones)
9111 4th Avenue West, Seattle, WA 98119

Geraniaceae (Robin Parer)
122 Hillcrest Avenue, Kentfield, CA 94904

Heronswood Nursery
7530 NE 288th Street, Kingston, WA 98346

Highfield Garden (Irene Moss)
4704 NE Cedar Creek Road, Woodland, WA 98674-2511

Lamb Nurseries
El01 Sharp Avenue, Spokane, WA 99202

Rain Forest Gardens (Elke and Ken Knechtel)
13139 224th Street RR2, Maple Ridge, BC V2X 7E7, Canada

AUSTRALIA
Coffields Nursery (Rene Coffield)
P0 Box 102, Cheswick, Victoria 3363

Digger's Garden Club (Clive Blazey)
105 La Trobe Parade, Dromana, Victoria 3936

Lambley Nursery (David Glenn)
PO Box 142, Olinda, Victoria 3788

Norgates Flower Farm (Denis Norgate)
Blackwood, Trentham Road, Victoria 3458

Rokewood Nursery (Felicity Kent)
Sims Road, Mt Barker, South Australia 5251

Romantic Cottage Gardens (Graham Cooke)
Bromany Brush, Boundary Road, Dromana, Victoria 3936

Viburnum Gardens (Michael Pitkin)
8 Sunnyridge Road, Arcadia, New South Wales 2159

Woodbank Nursery (Ken Gillanders)
RMB 303, Kingston, Tasmania 7150